The Greenprint:
Gods plan for cultivating land and people

Copyright © 2015 by David Obermiller

Published by David Obermiller
dobermiller@outlook.com

Compiler: David Obermiller
Editors: David Obermiller and Diana Santos
Layout and cover design by Eric Smalling

THE GREENPRINT

God's plan
for cultivating
land and
people

An Ellen White Compilation

Contents

Introduction

The Motivation for this Work

"A greater effort should be made to create and to encourage an interest in agricultural pursuits. Let the teacher call attention to what the Bible says about agriculture: that it was God's plan for man to till the earth; that the first man, the ruler of the whole world, was given a garden to cultivate; and that many of the world's greatest men, its real nobility, have been tillers of the soil. Show the opportunities in such a life." Education, pg. 218

This commission to teachers, found in Ellen White's seminal work on Christian education, planted the seed of conviction in my heart that a work such as this must be made available to the public. However, it took years to germinate; the soil of my mind not yet ready to support its growth. But God is a patient gardener! Frequently watered by the reminders of the Holy Spirit, and warmed by the rays of God's love for man, my soul finally became a fertile field in which this seed could grow. This work, the fruit of that divinely planted seed, is part of my effort to "create and encourage" more interest in agriculture. It is a work, I believe, long overdue.

The benefits of gardens and farms, outlined in the pages that follow, are truly as diverse as your backyard garden, touching all areas of life; the physical, mental, and spiritual. Yet, let none think that the garden offers her benefits to individuals alone; institutions of all types will find rich treasures in the ground. Thus, churches, schools, printing houses, hospitals, and conference offices are all counseled to participate in the act of cultivating the ground.

While Ellen White thoroughly enumerates the benefits of gardening, perhaps more significant is the emphasis she adds to the subject. It is not often that Ellen White describes the importance of a subject with such words and phrases as "essential," "the ABC of the educational work" of our schools, and describes those opposed to its implementation as unfit for school or conference employment because they would keep things from advancing in "right lines." But urgency is added to emphasis when she writes that the unwillingness to implement school farm programs has left us "far behind" in the "development of the third angels message." This should greatly concern those who wish to stand in the shadows of the tree of life, feasting on its monthly bonanza of fruit, sooner rather than later. This, not so subtly, indicates the impact farming is to have on the fulfillment of our prophetic mission. Thus, our desire to see the Master Gardener harvest the earth becomes the greatest motivation to "create and to encourage an interest in agricultural pursuits." Truly, from that perspective, this is a work long overdue!

Organization

The question may be asked, "Is this a book about gardening, farming, or agriculture? The answer is yes! All three terms are essentially exchangeable, each referring to the act of working the ground for the purpose of growing something, typically food, differing mostly with regard to the scale of the operation. Ellen White used all three words throughout her lifetime and I encourage the reader to view them as references to the same act on different scales; gardening the smallest, farming the largest, with agriculture being a more general term used to describe the cultivation of the ground. While it's true that you probably wouldn't call your backyard garden a farm, or a 1000 acre farm a garden, many of the benefits of cultivating the ground are the same regardless of the size of the operation. My hope is that the importance of the subject won't be lost on gardeners because Ellen White occasionally uses the words "farm" or "agriculture", and that farmers will keep listening for God's voice in these pages even when she speaks of "gardening".

Typically a compilation of Ellen White's material, regardless of the subject, would be arranged topically. For example, in the case of this work there could be chapters on "Gardening and Children," or "Gardening in Education," or "Hospital Gardens," etc. While this type of layout is convenient in some regards it also has some drawbacks. Alternatively, I have used a chronological layout with a user-friendly topical index at the end. This has several advantages.

The first is the elimination of particular statements being repeated over and over again throughout the work. Eliminating repetitive statements has allowed the inclusion of larger portions of the context surrounding a particular statement. This becomes the greatest advantage of this type of layout. Thus, Ellen White's counsels are presented in a threefold context. They first appear with the relevant context of the surrounding paragraphs. Secondly, they appear in relation to other statements she made in the surrounding months or years. This also allows the statements to be viewed within the context of events in church history at that time, which is crucial several times in this compilation. Lastly, it allows for the presentation of Ellen White's understanding of the topic to be seen from the beginning to the end of her ministry, a feature which I found to be particularly interesting.

This, I have hoped, would help eliminate the possibility of statements being taken out of context (misunderstood and misapplied), making the application of the principles involved easier.

One last comment is called for. This is a book without commentary. There are only two exceptions to this rule. The first is the occasional inclusion of notes that clarify the date at which certain statements were written by Ellen White. To avoid the natural repetition of statements that occurred within Sister White's lifetime the statements in this work were traced back to the source they originally appeared in. Sometimes this was a publication, sometimes a periodical, other times it was a personal letter, or a diary entry. Occasionally, notes were required to explain how the date of writing was identified. In a very few cases the date of writing is unknown beyond the year, or month it was written.

The only other commentary, if you'll call it that, is the inclusion of the dates at which certain Adventist institutions were opened, particularly schools. Since many of the counsels on farming are given within the context of education I have felt this was helpful to a proper understanding of more than one statement in the work.

David Obermiller

Timeline

1866 – Western Health Reform Institute Opened
(Later became Battle Creek Sanitarium)

1874 – Battle Creek College Founded (now Andrews University)

1882 – Healdsburg College (now Pacific Union College)

1882 – South Lancaster Academy Founded
(now Atlantic Union College)

1891 – Ellen White Leaves for Australia

1891 – Union College Founded

1892 – Walla Walla College Founded

1893 – Claremont Union College Founded
(now Helderberg College, South Africa)

1893 – Southern Training School opened
(now Southern Adventist University)

1893 – Keane Industrial Academy Founded (now Southwestern
Adventist University)

1896 – Oakwood Industrial School Founded

1897 – Avondale College Founded

1900 – (Aug. 29) Ellen White began her 23 day voyage back from
Australia

1901 – Battle Creek College Moved to Berrien Springs

1902 – Duncombe Hall Missionary College
(now Newbold) Founded

1904 – Nashville Agricultural and Normal Institute
(Madison) Opened

1904 – Washington Missionary College Opened
(now Washington Adventist University)

1909 – The College of Medical Evangelists Founded
(now Loma Linda)

1915 – (July 16) Death of Ellen White

1922 – La Sierra Academy Founded

Pre-Institutional Years (1864-1875)

1851

The Lord has shown me repeatedly, that it is contrary to the Bible to make any provision for our temporal wants in the time of trouble. I saw that if the saints had food laid up by them, or in the fields, in the time of trouble, when sword, famine and pestilence are in the land, it would be taken from them by violent hands, and strangers would reap their fields. Then will be the time for us to trust wholly in God, and he will sustain us. I saw that our bread and water would be sure at that time, and we should not lack or suffer hunger; for God was able to spread a table for us in the wilderness. And if necessary, he would send ravens to feed us as he did to feed Elijah, or rain manna from heaven, as he did for the Israelites. {ExV 44.1}

I saw that houses and lands would be of no use to the saints in the time of trouble, for they would then have to flee from their possessions, before infuriated mobs, and at that time they could not be disposed of to advance the cause of present truth. I was shown that it was the will of God that the saints should cut loose from every encumbrance before the time of trouble comes, and make a covenant with God by sacrifice. If they have their property on the altar, and earnestly inquire of God for duty, he will teach them when to dispose of these things. Then they will be free in the time of trouble, and have no clogs to weigh them down. {ExV 45.1}

I saw if any held on to their property, and did not inquire duty of the Lord, he would not make duty known, and they would be permitted to keep their property, and then in the time of trouble it would come up before them like a mountain to crush them, and they would try to dispose of it, but would not be able. I heard some mourn like this: "The cause was languishing, God's people were starving for the truth, and we made no effort to supply the lack, and now our property is useless. Oh! that we had let it go, and laid up treasure in heaven." I saw a sacrifice did not increase, but decrease, and was consumed. I also saw that God had not required all of his people to dispose of their property at the same time, but in a time of need he would teach them, if they desired to be taught, when to sell and how much to sell, and that some had been required to dispose of their property in time past to sustain the Advent cause, while he permitted others to keep theirs until a time of need. Then as the cause needs it, their duty is to sell. {ExV 45.2}

1864

Moses especially warned the children of Israel against being seduced into idolatry. He earnestly charged them to obey the commandments of God. If they would prove obedient, and love the Lord, and serve him with their undivided affections, he would give them rain in due season, and cause their vegetation to flourish, and increase their cattle. They should also enjoy especial and exalted privileges, and should triumph over their enemies. He related to them the advantages of the land of Canaan over that of Egypt. In certain seasons of the year, the cultivated lands in Egypt had to be watered from the river, by machinery, which was worked by the foot. This was a laborious process. {4aSG 54.1}

Moses said to them, "For the land, whither thou goest in to possess it, is not as the land of Egypt, from whence ye came out, where thou sowedst thy seed, and wateredst it with thy foot, as a garden of herbs. But the land, whither ye go to possess it, is a land of hills and valleys, and drinketh water of the rain of heaven. A land which the Lord thy God careth for. The eyes of the Lord thy God are always upon it, from the beginning of the year even unto the end of the year." {4aSG 54.2}

There are many inventions and improvements, and labor-saving machines now that the ancients did not have. They did not need them. The land has felt the curse, more and more heavily. Before the flood, the first leaf which fell, and was discovered decaying upon the ground, caused those who feared God great sorrow. They mourned over it as we mourn over the loss of a dead friend. In the decaying leaf they could see an evidence of the curse, and of the decay of nature. {4aSG 155.2}

The greater the length of time the earth has lain under the

curse, the more difficult has it been for man to cultivate it, and make it productive. As the soil has become more barren, and double labor has had to be expended upon it, God has raised up men with inventive faculties to construct implements to lighten labor on the land groaning under the curse. But God has not been in all man's inventions. Satan has controlled the minds of men to a great extent, and has hurried men to new inventions which has led them to forget God. {4aSG 155.3}

December 25, 1865

I saw the beneficial influence of outdoor labor upon those of feeble vitality and depressed circulation, especially upon women who have induced these conditions by too much confinement indoors. Their blood has become impure for want of fresh air and exercise. Instead of amusements to keep these persons indoors, care should be taken to provide outdoor attractions. I saw there should be connected with the Institute ample grounds, beautified with flowers and planted with vegetables and fruits. Here the feeble could find work, appropriate to their sex and condition, at suitable hours. These grounds should be under the care of an experienced gardener to direct all in a tasteful, orderly manner. {1T 562.2}

Note: The "Institute" here referred to was the Western Health Reform Institute, the first Adventist health institute. John Harvey Kellogg became the manager in 1876 and changed the name to Battle Creek Sanitarium a few months later.

1866 – Western Health Reform Institute Founded

April 14, 1868

Our skirts are few and light, not taxing our strength with the burden of many and longer ones. Our limbs being properly clothed, we need comparatively few; and these are suspended from the shoulders. Our dresses are fitted to sit easily, obstructing neither the circulation of the blood, nor natural, free, and full respiration. Our skirts being neither numerous nor fashionably long, do not impede the means of locomotion, but leave us to move about with ease and activity. All these things are necessary to health. {RH, April 14, 1868 par. 24}

Our limbs and feet are suitably protected from cold and damp, to secure the circulation of the blood to them, with all its blessings. We can take exercise in the open air, in the dews of morning or evening, or after the falling storm of snow or rain, without fears of taking cold. Morning exercise, in walking in the free, invigorating air of heaven, or cultivating flowers, small fruits, and vegetables, is necessary to a healthful circulation of the blood. It is the surest safeguard against colds, coughs, congestions of the brain and lungs, inflammation of the liver, the kidneys, and the lungs, and a hundred other diseases. {RH, April 14, 1868 par. 25}

If those ladies who are failing in health, suffering in consequence of these diseases, would lay off their fashionable robes, clothe themselves suitably for the enjoyment of such exercise, and move out carefully at first, as they can endure it, and increase the amount of exercise in the open air as it gives them strength to endure, and dismiss their doctors and drugs, most of them might recover health, to bless the world with their example and the work of their hands. If they would dress their daughters properly, they might live to enjoy health, and to bless others. {RH, April 14, 1868 par. 26}

Note: These paragraphs are taken from an article in the Review and Herald dealing with the subject of dress reform. Apparently, some of the dresses worn by women at the time of writing were heavy and cumbersome enough to prevent outdoor activity.

1869

You have been placed in unfavorable circumstances for the development of a good Christian character; but you are now placed where you may build up a reputation, or blast it. The latter we do not believe you will do. But you are not secure from temptation. In one single hour you may take a course which will afterward cost you bitter tears of repentance. By yielding to temptation, you may estrange hearts from you, lose the respect and esteem you have been acquiring from those around you, and also stain your Christian character. You have the lesson of submission to learn. You consider it beneath you to do duties about the house--chores and little errands. You have a positive dislike for these little requirements; but you should cultivate a love for these very things to which you are so averse. Until you do this, you will not be acceptable help anywhere. When engaged in these necessary small things, you are doing more real service than when engaged in large business and in laborious work. {2T 308.2}

I have a case now in mind of one who was presented before me in vision who neglected these little things and could not interest himself in small duties, seeking to lighten the work of those indoors; it was too small business. He now has a family, but he still possesses the same unwillingness to engage in these small yet important duties. The result is, great care rests upon his wife. She has to do many things, or they will be left undone; and the amount of care which comes upon her because of her husband's lack is breaking her constitution. He cannot now overcome this evil as easily as he could in his youth. He neglects the little duties and fails to keep everything up tidy and nice, therefore cannot make a successful farmer. "He that is faithful in that which is least is faithful also in much: and he that is unjust in the least is unjust also in much." {2T 309.1}

Note: The paragraphs above are portion of a letter written to a boy that had been raised in an orphanage.

March 29, 1870

It is displeasing to God for any who profess to love him to work so hard with their hands and brains in their own business as to unfit themselves to render to God that service which comes from a fervent spirit. Christians should not make it a practice to urge their families to work until their energy is exhausted, and there is no vitality left to devote to the service of God, who requires soul, body, mind, and strength. If you employ the powers of your entire being to serve your own interest, what have you reserved to offer to God? Is it not a lame sacrifice? "I beseech you, therefore, brethren, by the mercies of God, that ye present your bodies a living sacrifice, holy, acceptable unto God, which is your reasonable service." {RH, March 29, 1870 par. 16}

Time is well spent that is devoted to the instruction of your children. You may be living, acceptable missionaries for God, and yet be mechanics, merchants, and farmers. You can engage in the work of your Master with all your souls, and let your light shine to others. May the Lord arouse you, is my prayer, to seek first the kingdom of God and his righteousness, and all these things shall be added. How do you prove God? Have you not made all the provisions it was possible for you to make? Have you not looked far into the future to arrange for your supposed future wants? Have you not taken thought for the morrow, and is not your salvation made secondary? You do not attend to things of eternal moment; but are looking years into the future, to provide for your families. {RH, March 29, 1870 par. 17}

June 1, 1871

God designs we should draw lessons from nature, and make a practical application of these lessons to our own lives. Although we may suffer under disappointments, reverses, and affliction, yet we cannot afford to fret, and walk under a cloud, and cast a shadow upon all with whom we associate. Invalids may imitate nature. They need not be like a withered, decaying branch. Let vegetation, that is clothed in cheerful green, cheer and comfort you, and suggest to you the happiness that you may reflect upon others, by presenting before them the aspect of freshness and cheerfulness, instead of complaints, sighs, and groans, and apparent languor in every step, and an appearance of inability in every move. {HR, June 1, 1871 par. 8}

Live, dear invalid friends, while you do live, and train yourselves to shed fragrance like the fresh flowers. If you are burdened and weary, you need not curl up like leaves upon a withered branch. Cheerfulness and a clear conscience are better than drugs, and will be an effective agent in your restoration to health. In order for you to be cheerful, you should have exercise. You should have something useful to do. Invalid sisters should have something to call them out of doors, to work in the ground. This was the employment given by God to our first parents. God knew that employment was necessary to happiness. You should have a spot of ground to claim as yours, to tend and cultivate. You may have a pride in keeping out every weed, and may watch with interest the beautiful development of every leaf and opening bud and flower, and be charmed with the miracles of God seen in nature. As you view the shrubs and flowers, remember God loves the beautiful in nature. As you watch the harmonious colors of the various beautiful-tinted flowers of June, bear in mind that God loves the beautiful in human nature formed in his image.

A pure, harmonious character, a sunny temper, reflecting light and cheerfulness, glorifies God, and benefits humanity. Inspiration tells us that a meek and quiet spirit in the sight of God is of great price. {HR, June 1, 1871 par. 9}

As you cultivate your vegetables and flowers, and remove the weeds and prune from them the lifeless branches, bear in mind this is the work God is doing for you if he loves you. As you remove everything unsightly, and injurious to your plants, that nothing but the beautiful may appear, remember that just so God is doing with your human garden. He would discipline you, and would root out all the weeds, and all corruption and vileness, that you may possess a symmetrical character, and be free from evil habits, that you may not become sour, distrustful, and gloomy. {HR, June 1, 1871 par. 10}

1872

All the powers of the mind should be called into use and developed in order for men and women to have well-balanced minds. The world is full of one-sided men and women who have become such because one set of their faculties was cultivated while others were dwarfed from inaction. The education of most youth is a failure. They overstudy, while they neglect that which pertains to practical business life. Men and women become parents without considering their responsibilities, and their offspring sink lower in the scale of human deficiency than they themselves. Thus the race is fast degenerating. The constant application to study, as the schools are now conducted, is unfitting youth for practical life. The human mind will have action. If it is not active in the right direction, it will be active in the wrong. In order to preserve the balance of the mind, labor and study should be united in the schools. {3T 152.2}

Provision should have been made in past generations for education upon a larger scale. In connection with the schools should have been agricultural and manufacturing establishments. There should also have been teachers of household labor. And a portion of the time each day should have been devoted to labor, that the physical and mental powers might be equally exercised. If schools had been established upon the plan we have mentioned, there would not now be so many unbalanced minds. {3T 153.1}

God prepared for Adam and Eve a beautiful garden. He

provided for them everything that their wants required. He planted for them fruit-bearing trees of every variety. With a liberal hand He surrounded them with His bounties. The trees for usefulness and beauty, and the lovely flowers which sprang up spontaneously and flourished in rich profusion around them, were to know nothing of decay. Adam and Eve were rich indeed. They possessed Eden. Adam was lord in his beautiful domain. None can question the fact that he was rich. But God knew that Adam could not be happy unless he had employment. Therefore He gave him something to do; he was to dress the garden. {3T 153.2}

I have been led to inquire: Must all that is valuable in our youth be sacrificed in order that they may obtain a school education? Had there been agricultural and manufacturing establishments connected with our schools, and had competent teachers been employed to educate the youth in the different branches of study and labor, devoting a portion of each day to mental improvement and a portion to physical labor, there would now be a more elevated class of youth to come upon the stage of action to have influence in molding society. Many of the youth who would graduate at such institutions would come forth with stability of character. They would have perseverance, fortitude, and courage to surmount obstacles, and such principles that they would not be swayed by a wrong influence, however popular. There should have been experienced teachers to give lessons to young ladies in the cooking department. Young girls should have been instructed to manufacture wearing apparel, to cut, make, and mend garments, and thus become educated for the practical duties of life. {3T 155.2}

For young men there should be establishments where they could learn different trades which would bring into exercise their muscles as well as their mental powers. If the youth can have but a one-sided education, which is of the greater consequence, a knowledge of the sciences,--with all the disadvantages to health and life,--or a knowledge of labor for practical life? We unhesitatingly answer: The latter. If one must be neglected, let it be the study of books. {3T 156.1}

Men who have good physical powers should educate themselves to think as well as to act, and not depend upon others to be brains for them. It is a popular error with a large class to regard work as degrading. Therefore young men are very anxious to educate themselves to become teachers, clerks, merchants, lawyers, and to occupy almost any position that does not require physical labor. Young women regard housework as demeaning. And although the physical exercise required to perform household labor, if not too severe, is calculated to promote health, yet they will seek for an education that will fit them to become teachers or clerks, or will learn some trade which will confine them indoors to sedentary employment. The bloom of health fades from their cheeks, and disease fastens upon them, because they are robbed of physical exercise and their habits are perverted generally. All this because it is fashionable! They enjoy delicate life, which is feebleness and decay. {3T 158.1}

True, there is some excuse for young women not choosing housework for employment, because those who hire kitchen girls generally treat them as servants. Frequently their employers do not respect them and treat them as though they were unworthy to be members of their families. They do not give them the privileges they do the seamstress, the copyist, and the teacher of music. But there can be no employment more important than that of housework. To cook well, to present healthful food upon the table in an inviting manner, requires intelligence and experience. The one who prepares the food that is to be placed in our stomachs, to be converted into blood to nourish the system, occupies a most important and elevated position. The position of copyist, dressmaker, or music teacher cannot equal in importance that of the cook. {3T 158.2}

The foregoing is a statement of what might have been done by a proper system of education. Time is too short now to accomplish that which might have been done in past generations; but we can do much, even in these last days, to correct the existing evils in the education of youth. And because time is short, we should be in earnest and work zealously to give the young that education which is consistent with our faith. We are reformers. We desire that our children should study to the best advantage. In order to do this, employment should be given them which will call the muscles into exercise. Daily, systematic labor should constitute a part of the education of the youth, even at this late period. Much can now be gained by connecting labor with schools. In following this plan the students will realize elasticity of spirit and vigor of thought, and will be able to accomplish more mental labor in a given time than they could by study alone. And they can leave school with their constitutions unimpaired and with strength and courage to persevere in any position in which the providence of God may place them. {3T 158.3}

Because time is short, we should work with diligence and double energy. Our children may never enter college, but they can obtain an education in those essential branches which they can turn to a practical use and which will give culture to the mind and bring its powers into use. Very many youth who have gone through a college course have not obtained that true education that they can put to practical use. They may have the name of having a collegiate education, but in reality they are only educated dunces. {3T 159.1}

Note: As a matter of historical context the first Seventh-day Adventist school was started in 1872 in Battle Creek by Goodloe Harper Bell. This school would become Battle Creek College in 1874.

1874 – Battle Creek College Founded

The Battle Creek Years (1876-1890)

1876

Dear Brother E, you have made a great mistake in giving this world your ambition. You are exacting and sometimes impatient, and at times require too much of your son. He has become discouraged. At your house it has been work, work, work, from early morning until night. Your large farm has brought extra cares and burdens into your house. You have talked upon business; for business was primary in your mind, and "out of the abundance of the heart the mouth speaketh." Has your example in your family exalted Christ and His salvation above your farming interest and your desire for gain? If your children fail of everlasting life, the blood of their souls will surely be found on the garments of their father. {4T 48.1}

You have devoted so much time to missionary work which has no connection with our faith, and been so pressed with cares and responsibilities, that you have not kept pace with the work of God for this time, and have had little leisure to make the narrow precincts of home attractive to your children. You have not studied their needs, nor understood their active, developing minds; therefore you have withheld from them simple indulgences that would have gratified them without injury. It would have been a trifling tax upon you to give your children greater attention, and it would have been of the greatest value to them. {4T 136.2}

To live in the country would be very beneficial to them; an active, out-of-door life would develop health of both mind and body. They should have a garden to cultivate, where they might find both amusement and useful employment. The training of plants and flowers tends to the improvement of taste and judgment, while an acquaintance with God's useful and beautiful creations has a refining and ennobling influence upon the mind, referring it to the Maker and Master of all. {4T 136.3}

January 1, 1880

We should all be working together with God. No idlers are acknowledged as his servants. The members of the church should individually feel that the life and prosperity of the church is affected by their course of action. Those in the church who have sufficient talent to engage in any of the various vocations of life, such as teaching, building, manufacturing, and farming, will generally be prepared to labor for the upbuilding of the church by serving on committees or as teachers in Sabbath-schools, engaging in missionary labor or filling the different offices connected with the church. {RH, January 1, 1880 par. 7}

1880

Said Christ: "How hardly shall they that have riches enter into the kingdom of God!" And His disciples were astonished at His doctrine. When a minister who has labored successfully in securing souls to Jesus Christ abandons his sacred work in order to secure temporal gain, he is called an apostate, and he will be held accountable to God for the talents that he has misapplied. When men of business, farmers, mechanics, merchants, lawyers, etc., become members of the church, they become servants of Christ; and although their talents may be entirely different, their responsibility to advance the cause of God by personal effort, and with their means, is no less than that which rests upon the minister. The woe which will fall upon the minister if he preach not the gospel, will just as surely fall upon the businessman, if he, with his different talents, will not be a co-worker with Christ in accomplishing the same results. When this is brought home to the individual, some will say, "This is an hard saying;" nevertheless it is true, although continually contradicted by the practice of men who profess to be followers of Christ. {4T 468.3}

September 13, 1881

One of the surest safeguards for the young is useful occupation. Had they been trained to industrious habits, so that all their hours were usefully employed, they would have no time for repining at their lot or for idle day-dreaming. They would be in little danger of forming vicious habits or associations. Let the youth be taught from childhood that there is no excellence without great labor. Aspirations for eminence will not avail. Young friends, the mountain-top cannot be reached by standing still, and wishing yourselves there. You can gain your object only by taking one step at a time, advancing slowly perhaps, but holding every step gained. It is the energetic, persevering worker that will scale the Alps. Every youth should make the most of his talents, by improving to the utmost present opportunities. He who will do this, may reach almost any height in moral and intellectual attainments. But he must possess a brave and resolute spirit. He will need to close his ears to the voice of pleasure; he must often refuse the solicitations of young companions. He must stand on guard continually, lest he be diverted from his purpose. {RH, September 13, 1881 par. 5}

Many parents remove from their country homes to the city, regarding it as a more desirable or profitable location. But by making this change they expose their children to many and great temptations. The boys have no employment, and they obtain a street education, and go on from one step in depravity to another, until they lose all interest in anything that is good and pure and holy. How much better had the parents remained with their families in the country, where the influences are most favorable for physical and mental strength. Let the youth be taught to labor in tilling the soil, and let them sleep the sweet sleep of weariness and innocence {RH, September 13, 1881 par. 6}

November 8, 1881

Our Creator has bestowed his bounties upon man with a liberal hand. Were all these gifts of Providence wisely and temperately employed, poverty, sickness, and distress would be well-nigh banished from the earth. But alas, we see on every hand the blessings of God changed to a curse by the wickedness of men. There is no class guilty of greater perversion and abuse of his precious gifts than are those who employ the products of the soil in the manufacture of intoxicating liquors. The nutritive grains, the healthful, delicious fruits, are converted into beverages that pervert the senses and madden the brain. As a result of the use of these poisons, thousands of families are deprived of the comforts and even the necessaries of life, acts of violence and crime are multiplied, and disease and death hurry myriads of victims to a drunkard's grave. {RH, November 8, 1881 par. 1}

Note: This paragraph introduced an article that appeared in the Review and Herald that addressed the subject of liquor licenses.

December, 1881

Our college is designed of God to meet the advancing wants for this time of peril and demoralization. The study of books only cannot give students the discipline they need. A broader foundation must be laid. The college was not brought into existence to bear the stamp of any one man's mind. Teachers and principal should work together as brethren. They should consult together, and also counsel with ministers and responsible men, and, above all else, seek wisdom from above, that all their decisions in reference to the school may be such as will be approved of God. {5T 22.2}

To give students a knowledge of books merely is not the purpose of the institution. Such education can be obtained at any college in the land. I was shown that it is Satan's purpose to prevent the attainment of the very object for which the college was established. Hindered by his devices, its managers reason after the manner of the world and copy its plans and imitate its customs. But in thus doing, they will not meet the mind of the Spirit of God. {5T 22.3}

A more comprehensive education is needed, an education which will demand from teachers and principal such thought and effort as mere instruction in the sciences does not require. The character must receive proper discipline for its fullest and noblest development. The students should receive at college such training as will enable them to maintain a respectable, honest, virtuous standing in society, against the demoralizing influences which are corrupting the youth. {5T 23.1}

It would be well could there be connected with our college, land for cultivation and also workshops under the charge of men competent to instruct the students in the various departments of physical labor. Much is lost by a neglect to unite physical with mental taxation. The leisure hours of the students are often occupied with frivolous pleasures, which weaken physical, mental, and moral powers. Under the debasing power of sensual indulgence, or the untimely excitement of courtship and marriage, many students fail to reach that height of mental development which they might otherwise have attained. {5T 23.2}

1882 – Healdsburg College (PUC), and South Lancaster Academy Founded (AUC)

1882

I have been shown that many of our people are robbing the Lord in tithes and in offerings, and as the result His work is greatly hindered. The curse of God will rest upon those who are living upon God's bounties and yet close their hearts and do nothing or next to nothing to advance His cause. Brethren and sisters, how can the beneficent Father continue to make you His stewards, furnishing you with means to use for Him, when you grasp it all, selfishly claiming that it is yours! {5T 151.2}

Instead of rendering to God the means He has placed in their hands, many invest it in more land. This evil is growing with our brethren. They had before all they could well care for, but the love of money or a desire to be counted as well off as their neighbors leads them to bury their means in the world and withhold from God His just dues. Can we be surprised if they are not prospered? if God does not bless their crops and they are disappointed? Could our brethren remember that God can bless twenty acres of land and make them as productive as one hundred, they would not continue to bury themselves in lands, but would let their means flow into God's treasury. "Take heed," said Christ, lest at any time your hearts be overcharged with surfeiting, and drunkenness, and cares of this life." Satan is pleased to have you increase your farms and invest your means in worldly enterprises, for by so doing you not only hinder the cause from advancing, but by anxiety and overwork lessen your prospect for eternal life. {5T 151.3}

Note: These paragraphs only occur once in Ellen White's writings. Found in Testimonies for the Church volume 5, they are in an article addressing the issues of tithing. The exact date of their writing is not given.

June 29, 1882

The young naturally desire activity, and if they find no legitimate scope for their pent-up energies after the confinement of the schoolroom, they become restless and impatient of control, and thus are led to engage in the rude, unmanly sports that disgrace so many schools and colleges, and even to plunge into scenes of actual dissipation. Many of the youth who left their homes innocent, are corrupted by their associations at school. {FE 72.3}

Every institution of learning should make provision for the study and practice of agriculture and the mechanic arts. Competent teachers should be employed to instruct the youth in the various industrial pursuits, as well as in the several branches of study. While a part of each day is devoted to mental improvement, let a stated portion be given to physical labor, and a suitable time to devotional exercises and the study of the Scriptures. {FE 72.4}

This training would encourage habits of self-reliance, firmness, and decision. Graduates of such institutions would be prepared to engage successfully in the practical duties of life. They would have courage and perseverance to surmount obstacles, and firmness of principle that would not yield to evil influences. {FE 73.1}

If the youth can have but a one-sided education, which is of the greatest importance, the study of the sciences, with all the disadvantages to health and morals, or a thorough training in practical duties, with sound morals and good physical development? We unhesitatingly say, the latter. But with proper effort both may, in most cases, be secured. {FE 73.2}

Those who combine useful labor with study have no need of gymnastic exercises. And work performed in the open air is tenfold more beneficial to health than in-door labor. Both the mechanic and the farmer have physical exercise, yet the farmer is the healthier of the two. Nothing short of nature's invigorating air and sunshine will fully meet the demands of the system. The tiller of the soil finds in his labor all the movements that were ever practiced in the gymnasium. His movement-room is the open fields. The canopy of heaven is its roof, the solid earth its floor. Here he plows and hoes, sows and reaps. Watch him, as in "haying time" he mows and rakes, pitches and tumbles, lifts and loads, throws off, treads down, and stows away. These various movements call into action the bones, joints, muscles, sinews, and nerves of the body. His vigorous exercise causes full, deep, strong inspirations and exhalations, which expand the lungs and purify the blood, sending the warm current of life bounding through arteries and veins. A farmer who is temperate in all his habits, usually enjoys health. His work is pleasant to him. He has a good appetite. He sleeps well, and may be happy. {FE 73.3}

Contrast the condition of the active farmer with that of the student who neglects physical exercise. He sits in a close room, bending over his desk or table, his chest contracted, his lungs crowded. He cannot take full, deep inspirations. His brain is tasked to the utmost, while his body is as inactive as though he had no particular use for it. His blood moves sluggishly through the system. His feet are cold, his head hot. How can such a person have health? {FE 74.1}

Let the student take regular exercise that will cause him to breathe deep and full, taking into his lungs the pure invigorating air of heaven, and he will be a new being. It is not hard study that is destroying the health of students, so much as it is their disregard of nature's laws. {FE 74.2}

August, 1885

People were subject to misfortune, sickness, and loss of property the same then [ancient Israel] as now; but so long as they followed the instruction given by God there were no beggars among them, neither any who suffered for food. Their wise Governor, foreseeing that misfortune would befall some, made provision for them. When the people entered Canaan, the land was divided among them according to their numbers, and special laws were enacted to prevent any one person from joining field to field, and claiming as his, all the land that he desired, or had money to purchase. No one was allowed to choose the most fertile parts for himself, and leave the poor and less desirable portions for his brother; for this would cultivate selfishness and a spirit of oppression, and give cause for dissatisfaction, complaint, and dissension. {HS 164.4}

By the special direction of God, the land was divided by lot. After it had been thus divided, no one was to feel at liberty, either from a love of change or a desire to make money, to trade his estate; neither was he to sell his land unless compelled to do so on account of poverty. And then whenever he or any of his kindred might desire to redeem it, the one who had purchased it must not refuse to sell it. And if the poor man had no one to redeem it for him, and was unable to do so himself, in the year of jubilee it should revert to him, and he should have the privilege of returning to his home and again enjoying it. Thus the poor and unfortunate were ever to have an equal chance with their more fortunate neighbors. {HS 165.1}

More than this, the Israelites were instructed to sow and reap their fields for six successive years; but every seventh year they were commanded to let the land rest. Whatever grew of itself was to be gathered by the poor; and what they left, the beasts of the field were to eat. This was to impress the people with the fact that it was God's land which they were permitted to possess for a time; that he was the rightful owner, the original proprietor, and that he would have special consideration made for the poor and unfortunate. This provision was made to lessen suffering, to bring some ray of hope, to flash some gleam of sunshine, into the lives of the suffering and distressed. Is any such statute regarded in England? Far from it. The Lord set needy human beings before the beasts; but this order has been reversed there, and, compared with the poor, horses, dogs, and other dumb animals are treated as princes. In some localities the poor are forbidden to step out of the path to pick the wild flowers which grow in abundance in many of the open fields. Anciently a man when hungry was permitted to enter another man's field or vineyard and eat as much as he chose. Even Christ and his disciples plucked and ate of the corn through which they passed. But how changed the order of things now! {HS 165.2}

If the laws given by God had continued to be carried out, how different would be the present condition of the world, morally, spiritually, and temporally. Selfishness and self-importance would not be manifested as now; but each would cherish a kind regard for the happiness and welfare of others, and such wide-spread destitution and human wretchedness as is now seen in most parts of England and Ireland would not exist. Instead of the poorer classes being kept under the iron heel of oppression by the wealthy, instead of having other men's brains to think and plan for them in temporal as well as in spiritual things, they would have some chance for independence of thought and action. {HS 165.3}

December 15, 1885

God's word, the blessed guide, given to man declares concerning these great and grand rocky mountains that have stood the storm and tempest, the torrent and the roar of the winds, "The mountains shall depart, and the hills shall be removed, but His kindness shall not depart, neither shall the covenant of peace be removed from the heart that trusts in Him with perfect faith." The range of the mountains which cover so much space with barren rocks and eternal snows is a storehouse of fertility to the plains. The precious things of the valley are nourished from these everlasting mountains. The Alps of Europe are its glory. The treasures of the hills send their blessings to millions. We see numerous cataracts rushing from the tops of the mountains into the valleys beneath. {3MR 215.2}

Note: This paragraph was taken from an entry into Ellen White's diary on Dec. 15, 1885. At the time she was visiting Europe and was returning to Switzerland after having visited Italy for the first time. Her diary comments were largely about the grandeur of the Alps.

August 26, 1886

Young persons are naturally active, and if they find no legitimate scope for their pent-up energies after the confinement of the schoolroom, they become restless and impatient of control; they are thus led to engage in the rude, unmanly sports that disgrace so many schools and colleges, and even to plunge into scenes of dissipation. And many who leave their homes innocent, are corrupted by their associations at school. Much could be done to obviate these evils, if every institution of learning would make provision for manual labor on the part of the students,--for actual practice in agriculture and the mechanic arts. Competent teachers should be provided to instruct the youth in various industrial pursuits, as well as in their studies in the school room. While a part of each day is devoted to mental improvement and physical labor, devotional exercises and the study of the Scriptures should not be overlooked. {ST, August 26, 1886 par. 6}

Students trained in this manner would have habits of self-reliance, firmness, and perseverance, and would be prepared to engage successfully in the practical duties of life. They would have courage and determination to surmount obstacles, and moral stamina to resist evil influences. {ST, August 26, 1886 par. 7}

If young persons can have but one set of faculties disciplined, which is most important, the study of the sciences, with the disadvantages to health and morals under which such knowledge is usually obtained, or a thorough training in practical duties, with sound morals and good physical development? In most cases both may be secured if parents will take a little pains; but if both cannot be had, we would unhesitatingly decide in favor of the latter. {ST, August 26, 1886 par. 8}

Where useful labor is combined with study, there is no need of gymnastic exercises; and much more benefit is derived from work performed in the open air than from indoor exercise. The farmer and the mechanic each have physical exercise; yet the farmer is much the healthier of the two, for nothing short of the invigorating air and sunshine will fully meet the wants of the system. The farmer finds in his labor all the movements that were ever practiced in the gymnasium. And his movement room is the open fields; the canopy of heaven is its roof, and the solid earth its floor. A farmer who is temperate in all his habits usually enjoys good health. His work is pleasant; and his vigorous exercise causes full, deep, and strong inspirations and exhalations, which expand the lungs and purify the blood, sending the warm current of life bounding through arteries and veins. {ST, August 26, 1886 par. 9}

In what contrast to the habits of the active farmer are those of the student who neglects physical exercise. The student sits day after day in a close room, bending over his desk or table, his chest contracted, his lungs crowded. His brain is taxed to the utmost, while his body is inactive. He cannot take full, deep inspirations; his blood moves sluggishly; his feet are cold, his head hot. How can such a person have health? It is not hard study that is destroying the health of students, so much as it is their disregard of nature's laws. Let them take regular exercise that will cause them to breathe deep and full, and they will soon feel that they have a new hold on life. {ST, August 26, 1886 par. 10}

October 31, 1886

In this world we are to obtain a fitness for the higher world. God has left a trust with us, and he expects us to use all our faculties in helping and blessing our fellowmen. He calls for our best affections, our highest powers, and he is dishonored when we follow a course that brings weakness and disease upon the physical and mental powers. {3MR 114.1}

"Consider the lilies of the field, how they grow; they toil not, neither do they spin; and yet I say unto you, that even Solomon, in all his glory, was not arrayed like one of these." {3MR 114.2}

Let the mother take her children with her into the field or garden, and from the things of nature draw lessons that will point them to nature's God, and aid them in the struggle against evil. Let her point them to the lofty trees, the shrubs, and the carpet of green that covers the earth. Let her teach them how the lily, striking its roots down deep through the mire into the sand below, gains nourishment that enables it to send up a pure, beautiful blossom. Then let her show them how, by rejecting that which is impure, and choosing that which is pure, they may grow up into pure, noble men and women.... {3MR 114.3}

The children need to be given lessons that will nurture in them courage to resist evil. Point them from nature to nature's God, and they will thus become acquainted with the Creator. "How can I best teach my children to serve and glorify God," should be the question occupying the minds of parents. If all heaven is interested in the welfare of the human race, should not we be diligent to do all in our power for the welfare of our children? {3MR 114.4}

November 9, 1886

Persons who indulge the habit of story-reading make no progress mentally or morally. The time so devoted is worse than wasted. The gospel seed that is sown in the heart remains unfruitful, or is choked by the weeds sown by such reading. Seed that does not spring up and bear fruit loses its power of germinating. The fig-tree which bore no fruit was doomed to be cut down, condemned as an encumbrance to the very soil it occupied. God requires healthy growth of every tree in the garden of the Lord. But story-reading dwarfs the intellect. Childhood and youth are the time to begin to store the mind, but not with the chips and dirt found in modern newspapers and sensational literature. The mind should be guarded carefully. Nothing should be allowed to enter that will harm or destroy its healthy vigor. But to prevent this, it should be preoccupied with good seed, which, springing to life, will bring forth fruit-bearing branches. If all kinds of seed are sown--good and bad indiscriminately--the mind's soil will be impoverished and demoralized by a wild and noxious growth. Weeds of every kind will flourish, and good seed attain no growth at all. A field left uncultivated speedily produces a rank growth of thistles and tangled vines, which exhaust the soil and are worthless to the owner. The ground is full of seeds blown and carried by the wind from every quarter; and if it is left uncultivated, they spring up to life spontaneously, choking every precious fruit-bearing plant that is struggling for existence. If the field were tilled and sown to grain, these valueless weeds would be extinguished, and could not flourish. {RH, November 9, 1886 par. 6}

December 27, 1886 (Written from Basle, Switzerland).

I have been shown that there was not that being done which God has a right to expect of you in New York State to advance his cause and push forward the work, in wisely investing his entrusted talents. All the money is the Lord's. Why do you withhold from God that which is his own? There is not one hundredth part being done that ought to be done in your State. There is so great lack of faith and corresponding works that God cannot do much for you. The narrow faith, the narrow plans, are the limiting and binding about of the work. God will work for us just in accordance with our faith. At the slow rate our people in many States are working, it would take a temporal millennium to warn the world. The angels are holding the four winds that they should not blow until the world is warned, until a people has decided for the truth, the honest of heart have been convicted and converted. Their power, their influence, and their means will then flow in the missionary channel. This is putting out the money to the exchangers, that when the Master shall come his stewards may present the talents doubled in the ingathering of souls to Jesus Christ. But the wealthy farmers are some of them acting as if in the day of God the Lord only would require of them to present to him enriched, improved farms, building added to building, and they say, "Here Lord are thy talents; behold, I have gained all this possession." If the acres of their farms were so many precious souls saved to Jesus Christ, if their buildings were so many souls to be presented to the Master, then he could say to these men, "Well done, good and faithful servant." But you cannot take these improved farms, or these buildings into heaven. The fires of the last days will consume them. If you invest and bury your talents of means in these earthly treasures, your heart is on them, your anxiety is for them, your persevering labor is for them, your tact, your skill is cultivated to serve earthly, worldly possessions, and are not directed or employed upon heavenly things. And you come to look upon means invested for larger plans in extending the work as so much means lost which bring no returns. This is all a mistake, because the earthly is exalted above the eternal. While the heart is on earthly treasures it can only estimate such; it cannot appreciate the heavenly treasure. It is fully occupied just as the Devil wants it should be; and the eternal is eclipsed by the earthly. {PH039 4.2}

May 10, 1888

There is a large field for you to work in. Both of you can give short lectures in the parlor at stated times, which will be select but plain, upon the human body and how to treat this wonderful house the Lord has given us, which will aid you in your work as physicians as nothing else can. The people are ignorant, and need to be enlightened on almost every point of how to treat their own bodies. Then there will not need to be a dwelling upon the delicate diseases nearly as much. {13MR 371.1}

Tell those who are sick that if the hosts of those who are dyspeptics and consumptives could turn farmers they might overcome disease, dispense with drugs and doctors, and recover health. But farmers themselves must get educated to give heed to the laws of life and health by regulating their labor, even if there is some loss in their grain or the harvesting of crops. Farmers work too hard and too constantly, and violate the laws of God in their physical nature. This is the worst kind of economy. For a day he may accomplish more, yet in the end he is a loser by his ill management of himself. . . . {13MR 371.2}

Note: Written to J. E. Caldwell and J. S. Gibbs, both of whom were physicians at the St. Helena sanitarium.

September 17, 1889

To promote the assembling of the people for religious service, as well as to provide for the poor, a second tithe of all the increase was required. Concerning the first tithe, the Lord had declared, "I have given the children of Levi all the tenth in Israel." But in regard to the second he commanded, "Thou shalt eat before the Lord thy God, in the place which he shall choose to place his name there, the tithe of thy corn, of thy wine, and of thine oil, and the firstlings of thy herds and of thy flocks; that thou mayest learn to fear the Lord thy God always." This tithe, or its equivalent in money, they were for two years to bring to the place where the sanctuary was established. After presenting a thank-offering to God, and a specified portion to the priest, the offerers were to use the remainder for a religious feast, in which the Levite, the stranger, the fatherless, and the widow should participate. Thus provision was made for the thank-offerings and feasts at the yearly festivals, and the people were drawn to the society of the priests and Levites that they might receive instruction and encouragement in the service of God. Every third year, however, this second tithe was to be used at home, in entertaining the Levite and the poor, as Moses said, "That they may eat within thy gates, and be filled." This tithe would provide a fund for the uses of charity and hospitality. {RH, September 17, 1889 par. 1}

And further provision was made for the poor. There is nothing, after their recognition of the claims of God, that more distinguishes the laws given by Moses than the liberal, tender, and hospitable spirit enjoined toward the poor. Although God had promised greatly to bless his people, it was not his design that poverty should be wholly unknown among them. He declared that the poor should never cease out of the land. There would ever be those among his people who would call into exercise their sympathy, tenderness, and benevolence. Then, as now, persons were subject to misfortune, sickness, and loss of property; yet so long as they followed the instruction given by God, there were no beggars among them, neither any who suffered for food. {RH, September 17, 1889 par. 2}

The law of God gave the poor a right to a certain portion of the produce of the soil. When hungry, a man was at liberty to go to his neighbor's field or orchard or vineyard, and eat of the grain or fruit to satisfy his hunger. It was in accordance with this permission that Jesus and his disciples plucked and ate of the standing grain as they passed through the field on the Sabbath day. {RH, September 17, 1889 par. 3}

All the gleanings of harvest-field, orchard, and vineyard, belonged to the poor. "When thou cuttest down thine harvest in thy field," said Moses, "and hast forgot a sheaf in the field, thou shalt not go again to fetch it. . . . When thou beatest thine olive tree, thou shalt not go over the boughs again. . . . When thou gatherest the grapes of thy vineyard, thou shalt not glean it afterward. It shall be for the stranger, for the fatherless, and for the widow. And thou shalt remember that thou wast a bondman in the land of Egypt." {RH, September 17, 1889 par. 4}

Every seventh year, special provision was made for the poor. The sabbatical year, as it was called, began at the end of the harvest. At the seed-time, which followed the ingathering, the people were not to sow. They should not dress the vineyard in the spring, and they must expect neither harvest nor vintage. Of that which the land produced spontaneously, they might eat while fresh, but they were not to lay up any portion of it in their store-houses. The yield of this year was to be free for the stranger, the Fatherless, and the widow, and even for the creatures of the field. {RH, September 17, 1889 par. 5}

But if the land ordinarily produced only enough to supply the wants of the people, how were they to subsist during the year when no crops were gathered? For this the promise of God made ample provision. "I will command my blessing upon you in the sixth year," he said, "and it shall bring forth fruit for three years. And ye shall sow the eighth year, and eat yet of old fruit until the ninth year; until her fruits come in ye shall eat of the old store." {RH, September 17, 1889 par. 6}

The observance of the sabbatical year was to be a benefit to both the land and the people. The soil, lying untilled for one season, would afterward produce more plentifully. The people were released from the pressing labors of the field; and while there were various branches of work that could be followed during this time, all enjoyed greater leisure, which afforded opportunity for the restoration of their physical powers for the exertions of the following years. They had more time for meditation and prayer, for acquainting themselves with the teachings and requirements of the Lord, and for the instruction of their households. {RH, September 17, 1889 par. 7}

February 16, 1890

I shall have to apologize for delaying to answer your letter. It seemed to be my duty to attend the ministerial institute, and to speak to the brethren assembled there. Then I am under the necessity of keeping four workers busy on different kinds of books. This with my much letter writing seems to keep me employed from three o'clock A.M. till seven o'clock P.M. I deeply sympathize with you, my brother, in your perplexities and trials. As to praying for the sick, it is too important a matter to be handled carelessly. I believe we should take everything to the Lord, and make known to God all our weaknesses, and specify all our perplexities. When in sorrow, when uncertain as to what course to pursue, two or three who are accustomed to pray should unite together in asking the Lord to let His light shine upon them, and to impart His special grace; and He will respect their petitions, He will answer their prayers. If we are under infirmities of body it is certainly consistent to trust in the Lord, making supplications to our God in our own case, and if we feel inclined to ask others in whom we have confidence, to unite with us in prayer to Jesus who is the mighty Healer, help will surely come if we ask in faith. I think we are altogether too faithless, too cold and lukewarm. {PC 28.1}

I understand the text in James is to be carried out when a person is sick upon his bed; if he calls for the elders of the church, and they carry out the directions in James, anointing the sick with oil, in the name of the Lord, praying over him the prayer of faith. We read, "The prayer of faith shall save the sick, and the Lord shall raise him up; and if he hath committed sins, they shall be forgiven him." It cannot be our duty to call for the elders of the church for every little ailment we have, for this would be putting a task upon the elders. If all should do this, their time would be fully employed,--they could do nothing else; but the Lord gives us the privilege of seeking Him individually in earnest prayer, of unburdening our souls to Him, keeping nothing from Him who has invited us, "Come unto me, all ye who are weary and heavy laden, and I will give you rest." O how grateful we should be that Jesus is willing and able to bear all our infirmities and strengthen and heal all our diseases if it will be for our good and for His glory. Some died in the days of Christ and in the days of the apostles because the Lord knew just what was best for them. I would not speak one word to lessen your faith and perplex and worry you. There is never danger of our being too much in earnest and having too much confidence and trust in God. Be of good courage; look to Jesus constantly. {PC 28.2}

Now in regard to that which we can do for ourselves. There is a point that requires careful, thoughtful consideration. I must become acquainted with myself, I must be a learner always as to how to take care of this building, the body God has given me, that I may preserve it in the very best condition of health. I must eat those things which will be for my very best good physically, and I must take special care to have my clothing such as will conduce to a healthful circulation of the blood. I must not deprive myself of exercise and air. I must get all the sunlight that it is possible for me to obtain. I must have wisdom to be a faithful guardian of my body. I should do a very unwise thing to enter a cool room when in a perspiration; I should show myself an unwise steward to allow myself to sit in a draught, and thus expose myself so as to take cold. I should be unwise to sit with cold feet and limbs and thus drive back the blood from the extremities to the brain or internal organs. I should always protect my feet in damp weather. I should eat regularly of the most healthful food which will make the best quality of blood, and I should not work intemperately if it is in my power to avoid doing so. And when I violate the laws God has established in my being, I am to repent and reform, and place myself in the most favorable condition under the doctors God has provided,--pure air, pure water, and the healing, precious sunlight. Water can be used in many ways to relieve suffering. Draughts of clear, hot water, taken before eating (half a quart, more or less), will never do any harm, but will rather be productive of good. A cup of tea made from catnip herb will quiet the nerves. Hop tea will induce sleep. Hop poultices over the stomach will relieve pain. If the eyes are weak, if there is pain in the eyes, or inflammation, soft flannel clothes wet in hot water and salt, will bring relief quickly. When the head is congested, if the feet and limbs are put in a bath with a little mustard, relief will be obtained. There are many more simple remedies which will do much to restore healthful action to the body. All these simple preparations the Lord expects us to use for ourselves, but man's extremities are God's opportunities. If we neglect to do that which is within the reach of nearly every family, and ask the Lord to relieve pain, when we are too indolent to make use of these remedies within our power, it is simply presumption. The Lord expects us to work in order that we obtain food. He does not propose that we shall gather the harvest unless we break the sod, till the soil, and cultivate the produce. Then God sends the rain and the sunshine and the clouds to cause vegetation to flourish. God works and man cooperates with God. Then there is seed time and harvest. God has caused to grow out of the ground, herbs for the use of man, and if we understand the nature of those roots and herbs, and make a right use of them, there would not be a necessity of running for the doctor, so frequently, and people would be in much better health than they are today. I believe in calling upon the Great Physician when we have used the remedies I have mentioned. In regard to manner of labor, we certainly need to be wise as serpents and harmless as doves. We might be very zealous, but it might be an unwise zeal, and serve to hedge up our way. Then there is danger of being so circumscribed in our work as to do very little good. {PC 28.3}

1891 – Ellen White Leaves for Australia, Union College Founded

1892 – Walla Walla College Founded

The Australian Years (1891-1901)

Introductory Note: In the fall of 1891 Ellen White headed to Australia where she would live until late in the summer of 1900. All of the statements in this section were written from Australia during this time period.

1892

How many useful and honored workers in God's cause have received a training amid the humble duties of the most lowly positions in life. Moses was the prospective ruler of Egypt, but God could not take him from the king's court to do the work appointed him. Only when he had been for forty years a faithful shepherd was he sent to be the deliverer of his people. Gideon was taken from the threshing of wheat to be the instrument in the hands of God for delivering the armies of Israel. Elisha was called to leave the plow and do the bidding of God. Amos was husbandman, a tiller of the soil, when God gave him a message to proclaim. {GW92 316.1}

These lessons should be kept in view by those who have to do with the training of workers for the cause of God. All who become co-workers with Christ will have a great deal of hard, uncongenial labor to perform, and their lessons of instruction should be wisely chosen, and adapted to their peculiarities of character, and the work which they are to pursue. {GW92 317.1}

1893 – Southern Training School (Graysville) Opened

February 14, 1893

I have been deeply interested in the relation of a recent experience of Elder Daniells, who, on his way from Melbourne to Adelaide, stopped at a town called Nhill, to visit some young men who have been sending in orders to the Echo office for our papers and books. He found here a young man by the name of Hansen, a Dane, who chanced upon the Echo at a public library, and became an interested reader of the paper. The subjects of truth presented in its columns found a place in his heart, and he began to talk about them to a friend at the hotel where he was in service. This man, Mr. Williams, also became interested, and they sent in orders for other publications, becoming regular subscribers to the paper. Elder Daniells found them eager for a better knowledge of the truth. Upon the table of Mr. Williams was found "Thoughts on Daniel and the Revelation," and several other books published by our people. They had seen but one man who was of our faith. They bought from Elder Daniells three copies of "Steps to Christ," so that they might have one apiece, and another to give to a minister. Elder Daniells was pleased with his visit, and encouraged by his conversation with these inquirers after truth. {RH, February 14, 1893 par. 1}

These men had studied the truth from the printed page and the Bible, and had accepted all points of doctrine as far as they could understand them without the aid of the living preacher. A great work is going silently on through the distribution of our publications; but what a great amount of good might be done if some of our brethren and sisters from America would come to these colonies, as fruit-growers, farmers, or merchants, and in the fear and love of God, would seek to win souls to the truth. If such families were consecrated to God, he would use them as his agents. Ministers have their place and their work, but there are scores that the minister cannot reach, who might be reached by families who could visit with the people and impress upon them the truth for these last days. In their domestic or business relations they could come in contact with a class who are inaccessible to the minister, and they could open to them the treasures of the truth, and impart to them a knowledge of salvation. There is altogether too little done in this line of missionary work; for the field is large, and many workers could labor with success in this line of effort. If those who have received a knowledge of the truth had realized the necessity of studying the Scriptures for themselves, if they had felt the weight of responsibility that rests upon them, as faithful stewards of the grace of God, they would have brought light to many who sit in darkness, and what a harvest of souls would have been gathered for the Master. If each one realized his accountability to God for his personal influence, he would in no case be an idler, but would cultivate his ability, and train every power that he might serve him who has purchased him with his own blood. {RH, February 14, 1893 par. 2}

1894 – Keen Industrial Academy Opened

February, 1894

Australia needs the leaven of sound, solid, common sense to be freely introduced into all her cities and towns. There is need of proper education. Schools should be established for the purpose of obtaining not only knowledge from books, but knowledge of practical industry. Men are needed in different communities to show the people how riches are to be obtained from the soil. The cultivation of land will bring its return. {SpTEd 92.1}

Through the observance of holidays the people both of the world and of the churches have been educated to believe that these lazy days are essential to health and happiness; but the results reveal that they are full of evil, which is ruining the country. The youth generally are not educated to diligent habits. Cities and even country towns are becoming like Sodom and Gomorrah, and like the world in the days of Noah. The training of the youth in those days was after the same order as children are being educated and trained in this age, to love excitement, to glorify themselves, to follow the imagination of their own evil hearts. Now as then, depravity, cruelty, violence, and crime are the result. {SpTEd 92.2}

All these things are lessons for us. Few now are really industrious and economical. Poverty and distress are on every hand. There are men who work hard, and obtain very little for their labor. There is need of much more extensive knowledge in regard to the preparation of the soil. There is not sufficient breadth of view as to what can be realized from the earth. A narrow and unvarying routine is followed with discouraging results. The land boom has cursed this country, extravagant prices have been paid for lands bought on credit; then the land must be cleared, and more money is hired; a house to be built calls for more money, and then interest with open mouth swallows up all the profits. Debts accumulate, and then come the closing and failures of banks, and then the foreclosure of mortgages. Thousands have been turned out of employment; families lose their little all; they borrow and borrow, and then have to give up their property and come out penniless. Much money and hard labor have been put into farms bought on credit, or inherited with an incumbrance. The occupants lived in hope of becoming real owners, and it might have been so, but for the failure of banks throughout the country. {SpTEd 93.1}

Now the case where a man owns his place clear is a happy exception to the rule. Merchants are failing, families are suffering for food and clothing. No work presents itself. But the holidays are just as numerous. Their amusements are entered into as eagerly. All who can do so will spend their hard-earned pence and shillings and pounds for a taste of pleasure, for strong drink, or some other indulgence. The papers that report the poverty of the people, have regular standing notices of the horse-races, and of the prizes presented for different kinds of exciting sports. The shows, the theaters, and all such demoralizing amusements, are taking the money from the country, and poverty is continually increasing. Poor men will invest their last shilling in a lottery, hoping to secure a prize, and then they have to beg for food to sustain life, or go hungry. Many die of hunger, and many put an end to their existence. The end is not yet. Men take you to their orchards of oranges and lemons, and other fruits, and tell you that the produce does not pay for the work done in them. It is next to impossible to make ends meet, and parents decide that the children shall not be farmers; they have not the courage and hope to educate them to till the soil. {SpTEd 94.1}

What is needed is schools to educate and train the youth so that they will know how to overcome this condition of things. There must be education in the sciences, and education in plans and methods of working the soil. There is hope in the soil, but brain and heart and strength must be brought into the work of tilling it. The money devoted to horse-racing, theater-going, gambling, and lotteries; the money spent in the public houses for beer and strong drink,--let it be expended in making the land productive, and we shall see a different state of things. {SpTEd 94.2}

This country needs educated farmers. The Lord gives the showers of rain and the blessed sunshine. He gives to men all their powers; let them devote heart and mind and strength to doing his will in obedience to his commandments. Let them cut off every pernicious habit, never expending a penny for beer or liquor of any kind, nor for tobacco, having nothing to do with horse-racing or similar sports, and then commit themselves to God, working with their endowment of physical strength, and their labor will not be in vain. That God who has made the world for the benefit of man, will provide means from the earth to sustain the diligent worker. The seed placed in thoroughly prepared soil, will produce its harvest. God can spread a table for his people in the wilderness. {SpTEd 95.1}

The various trades and occupations have to be learned, and they call into exercise a great variety of mental and physical capabilities; the occupations requiring sedentary habits are the most dangerous, for they take men away from the open air and sunshine, and train one set of faculties, while other organs are becoming weak from inaction. Men carry on their work, perfect their business, and soon lie down in the grave. Much more favorable is the condition of one whose occupation keeps him in the open air, exercising his muscles, while the brain is equally taxed, and all the organs have the privilege of doing their work. To those who can live outside of the cities, and labor in the open air, beholding the works of the great Master Artist, new scenes are continually unfolding. As they make the book of nature their study, a softening, subduing influence comes over them; for they realize that God's care is over all, from the glorious sun in the heavens to the little brown sparrow or the tiniest insect that has life. The Majesty of heaven has pointed us to these things of God's creation as an evidence of his love. He who fashioned the flowers has said: "Behold the lilies of the field, how they grow; they toil not, neither do they spin; and yet I say unto you that even Solomon in all his glory was not arrayed like one of these. Wherefore if God so clothe the grass of the field, which today is, and tomorrow is cast into the oven, shall he not much more clothe you, O ye of little faith?" The Lord is our teacher, and under his instruction we may learn the most precious lessons from nature. {SpTEd 95.2}

When students enter the school to obtain an education, the instructors should endeavor to surround them with objects of the most pleasing, interesting character, that the mind may not be confined to the dead study of books. The school should not be in or near a city, where its extravagance, its wicked pleasures, its wicked customs and practices will require constant work to counteract the prevailing iniquity, that it may not poison the very atmosphere which the students breathe. All schools should be located, so far as possible, where the eye will rest upon the things of nature instead of clusters of houses. The ever-shifting scenery will gratify the taste, and control the imagination. Here is a living teacher, instructing constantly. {SpTEd 98.2}

I have been troubled over many things in regard to our school. In their work the young men are associated with the young women, and are doing the work which belongs to women. This is nearly all that can be found for them to do as they are now situated; but from the light given me, this is not the kind of education that the young men need. It does not give them the knowledge they need to take with them to their homes. There should be a different kind of labor opened before them, that would give opportunity to keep the physical powers taxed equally with the mental. There should be land for cultivation. The time is not far distant when the laws against Sunday labor will be more stringent, and an effort should be made to secure grounds away from the cities, where fruits and vegetables can be raised. Agriculture will open resources for self-support, and various other trades also could be learned. This real, earnest work calls for strength of intellect as well as of muscle. Method and tact are required even to raise fruits and vegetables successfully. And habits of industry will be found an important aid to the youth in resisting temptation. {SpTEd 99.1}

Here is opened a field to give vent to their pent-up energies, that, if not expended in useful employment, will be a continual source of trial to themselves and to their teachers. Many kinds of labor adapted to different persons may be devised. But the working of the land will be a special blessing to the worker. There is a great want of intelligent men to till the soil, who will be thorough. This knowledge will not be a hindrance to the education essential for business or for usefulness in any line. To develop the capacity of the soil requires thought and intelligence. Not only will it develop muscle, but capability for study, because the action of brain and muscle is equalized. We should so train the youth that they will love to work upon the land, and delight in improving it. The hope of advancing the cause of God in this country is in creating a new moral taste in love of work, which will transform mind and character. {SpTEd 99.2}

False witness has been borne in condemning land which, if properly worked, would yield rich returns. The narrow plans, the little strength put forth, the little study as to the best methods, call loudly for reform. The people need to learn that patient labor will do wonders. There is much mourning over unproductive soil, when if men would read the Old Testament Scriptures they would see that the Lord knew much better than they in regard to the proper treatment of land. After being cultivated for several years, and giving her treasure to the possession of man, portions of the land should be allowed to rest, and then the crops should be changed. We might learn much also from the Old Testament in regard to the labor problem. If men would follow the directions of Christ in regard to remembering the poor and supplying their necessities, what a different place this world would be! {SpTEd 100.1}

Let God's glory be kept ever in view; and if the crop is a failure, be not discouraged; try again; but remember that you can have no harvest unless the ground is properly prepared for the seed; failure may be wholly due to neglect on this point. {SpTEd 101.1}

The school to be established in Australia should bring the question of industry to the front, and reveal the fact that physical labor has its place in God's plan for every man, and that his blessing will attend it. The schools established by those who teach and practice the truth for this time, should be so conducted as to bring fresh and new incentives into all kinds of practical labor. There will be much to try the educators, but a great and noble object has been gained when students shall feel that love for God is to be revealed, not only in the devotion of heart and mind and soul, but in the apt, wise appropriation of their strength. Their temptations will be far less; from them by precept and example a light will radiate amid the erroneous theories and fashionable customs of the world. Their influence will tend to correct the false idea that ignorance is the mark of a gentleman. {SpTEd 101.2}

God would be glorified if men from other countries who have acquired an intelligent knowledge of agriculture, would come to this land, and by precept and example teach the people how to cultivate the soil, that it may yield rich treasures. Men are wanted to educate others how to plow, and how to use the implements of agriculture. Who will be missionaries to do this work, to teach proper methods to the youth, and to all who feel willing and humble enough to learn? If any do not want you to give them improved ideas, let the lessons be given silently, showing what can be done in setting out orchards and planting corn; let the harvest be eloquent in favor of right methods of labor. Drop a word to your neighbors when you can, keep up the culture of your own land, and that will educate. {SpTEd 101.3}

It may be urged by some that our school must be in the city in order to give influence to our work, and that if it is in the country, the influence is lost to the cities; but this is not necessarily the case. {SpTEd 102.1}

The youth who attend our school for the first time, are not prepared to exert a correct influence in any city as lights shining amid the darkness. They will not be prepared to reflect light until the darkness of their own erroneous education is dispelled. In the future our school will not be the same as it has been in the past. Among the students there have been reliable, experienced men who have taken advantage of the opportunity to gain more knowledge in order to do intelligent work in the cause of God. These have been a help in the school, for they have been as a balance-wheel; but in the future the school will consist mostly of those who need to be transformed in character, and who will need to have much patient labor bestowed upon them; they have to unlearn, and learn again. It will take time to develop the true missionary spirit, and the farther they are removed from the cities and the temptations that are flooding them, the more favorable will it be for them to obtain the true knowledge and develop well-balanced characters. {SpTEd 102.2}

Farmers need far more intelligence in their work. In most cases it is their own fault if they do not see the land yielding its harvest. They should be constantly learning how to secure a variety of treasures from the earth. The people should learn as far as possible to depend upon the products that they can obtain from the soil. In every phase of this kind of labor they can be educating the mind to work for the saving of souls for whom Christ has died. "Ye are God's husbandry; ye are God's building." Let the teachers in our schools take their students with them into the gardens and fields, and teach them how to work the soil in the very best manner. It would be well if ministers who labor in word or doctrine could enter the fields and spend some portion of the day in physical exercise with the students. They could do as Christ did in giving lessons from nature to illustrate Bible truth. Both teachers and students would have much more healthful experience in spiritual things, and much stronger minds and purer hearts to interpret eternal mysteries, than they can have while studying books so constantly, and working the brain without taxing the muscles. God has given men and women reasoning powers, and he would have men employ their reason in regard to the use of their physical machinery. The question may be asked, How can he get wisdom that holdeth the plow, and driveth oxen?--By seeking her as silver, and searching for her as for hid treasures. "For his God doth instruct him to discretion, and doth teach him." "This also cometh forth from the Lord of Hosts, which is wonderful in counsel, and excellent in working. {SpTEd 102.3}

He who taught Adam and Eve in Eden how to tend the garden, would instruct men today. There is wisdom for him who holds the plow, and plants and sows the seed. The earth has its concealed treasures, and the Lord would have thousands and tens of thousands working upon the soil who are crowded into the cities to watch for a chance to earn a trifle; in many cases that trifle is not turned into bread, but is put into the till of the publican, to obtain that which destroys the reason of man formed in the image of God. Those who will take their families into the country, place them where they have fewer temptations. The children who are with parents that love and fear God, are in every way much better situated to learn of the Great Teacher, who is the source and fountain of wisdom. They have a much more favorable opportunity to gain a fitness for the kingdom of heaven. Send the children to schools located in the city, where every phase of temptation is waiting to attract and demoralize them, and the work of character building is tenfold harder for both parents and children. {SpTEd 103.1}

The earth is to be made to give forth its strength; but without the blessing of God it could do nothing. In the beginning, God looked upon all that he had made, and pronounced it very good. The curse was brought upon the earth in consequence of sin. But shall this curse be multiplied by increasing sin? Ignorance is doing its baleful work. Slothful servants are increasing the evil by their lazy habits. Many are unwilling to earn their bread by the sweat of their brow, and they refuse to till the soil. But the earth has blessings hidden in her depths for those who have courage and will and perseverance to gather her treasures. Fathers and mothers who possess a piece of land and a comfortable home are kings and queens. {SpTEd 104.1}

Many farmers have failed to secure adequate returns from their land because they have undertaken the work as though it was a degrading employment; they do not see that there is a blessing in it for themselves and their families. All they can discern is the brand of servitude. Their orchards are neglected, the crops are not put in at the right season, and a mere surface work is done in cultivating the soil. Many neglect their farms in order to keep holidays and to attend horse-races and betting clubs; their money is expended in shows and lotteries and idleness, and then they plead that they cannot obtain money to cultivate the soil and improve their farms; but had they more money, the result would still be the same. {SpTEd 105.1}

May 29, 1894

"Much might be done in this country if there were those who would settle in different localities and cultivate the land as they do in America. Then they would be comparatively independent of the hard times. I think this will be brought about. Most diligent search has been made for a tract of land of several hundred acres on which to locate the school, so that the students may have an opportunity to till the soil, and poor families may have a little piece of land on which to grow vegetables and fruit. This would go far toward sustaining them, and they would have a chance to school their children. But money matters are very close. The people are all hard pressed for means, and know not just what to do unless times change. We must live and have means to carry forward the work. {RH, May 29, 1894 par. 6}

August 26, 1894

In this out-of-the-way place they found a pretty location, and people who were communicative and courteous. A pleasant-faced, white-haired, aged lady stated that they had lived there 32 years. She said that when her husband was alive he had kept the farm in good condition, but that since his death her son had neglected the work, and the farm did not look as it used to; for her son took no interest in farming. {13MR 349.1}

We should judge that the general difficulty with farming here is a lack of interest. There is plenty of idleness, [with] numerous holidays which are improved in following many kinds of objectionable amusements. The people are interested in horse-racing and card playing, in smoking and drinking, and this kind of employment benefits neither themselves nor others. They pass away their time in this way, and the lands are neglected. But if the soil were cultivated, it would produce excellent fruit. {13MR 349.2}

Because of the slack, slipshod way the landholders cultivate their farms, nothing flourishes as it should, and the impression made upon those who view the land is that it is too poor to yield a good crop. I have been anxious that the land should be taken in hand and thoroughly worked. Even the orange trees are left to grow up amid the grass, as wild trees grow. But where such immense trees flourish as flourish here, many of them growing up perfectly straight toward heaven, I am convinced that with the blessing of God, with diligence and faithfulness in working the land, farmers might produce gratifying results, and in return for the labor put forth they might reap a good harvest. {13MR 349.3}

I have thought of the many families who are crowded in our large cities, and I have thought how pleased I would be if some of them would come to this place, and put forth their energies in clearing the land and in subduing and cultivating the soil. This place is very restful to me. {13MR 350.1}

Sabbath, August 25, we all went out on the school land, and made ourselves comfortable in the woods. I had my folding chair; Brother Lawrence made a seat for his wife; and Brother Tucker and others seated themselves on the four rugs on the ground. I read two articles to them in which they seemed much interested. We then sang a hymn, and had a season of prayer. After we had eaten some oranges, we returned home. We all had a good appetite for our dinner. We enjoyed being on the school land amid the trees and the beautiful things of nature. I love to be in the groves where I can hear the birds sing. {13MR 350.2}

On Sunday, August 26, Brother Lawrence took us in the trap, and we drove over a good share of the school land, in order to obtain a more extensive view of the grounds. In some places the roads were rough; but I kept thinking, Let the cart jolt; it is a change of exercise; it will do me good. I enjoyed the trip, and we were out roughing it nearly all day. We came home at dark. {13MR 350.3}

I was much pleased with the ground. We walked over one farm where the land had been cleared, and which joined the school land. We examined the way in which they work the land, and found that the plough had been put in only to about the depth of six inches. An intelligent American farmer would not regard this as a faithful way of working the land. Those who work in this cheap, superficial way cannot expect to receive anything out of harmony with their method, but in accordance with it. {13MR 350.4}

Of this 40 acres only a portion of it had been cleared. We saw that during the previous year corn had been raised. There were fruit trees on the farm, and the peach trees were so full of blossoms that they looked like immense bouquets. First class lemons grow here. There are some lemons already on the trees; but it is a wonder that they have any trees at all. In order to clear the ground of weeds, they set fire to the underbrush, and from the appearance I should suppose that they had left the fire to run, for several of their fruitful lemon trees were so burned that they will probably die. {13MR 351.1}

The more I see the school property the more I am amazed at the cheap price at which it has been purchased. When the board want to go back on this purchase, I pledge myself to secure the land. I will settle it with poor families; I will have missionary families come out from America and do the best kind of missionary work in educating the people as to how to till the soil and make it productive. I have planned what can be raised in different places. I have said, "Here can be alfalfa, there can be strawberries, here can be sweet corn and common corn, and this ground will raise good potatoes, while that will raise good fruit of all kinds." So in imagination I have all the different places in flourishing condition. {13MR 351.2}

No one need to have regret in reference to this land; for with proper working it will surprise the people in this section of the country. All the regret I have is that we have not money to take in sections of the land that would extend the ground. I have not one doubt in reference to the securing of this land. If the Lord prospers those who occupy it and who cultivate it, as we believe He will, we shall see a change that will surprise all who look upon it. I can hardly endure the thought that time is passing, and that the work of clearing the land is delayed. {13MR 352.1}

I have walked over the most of the O'Leary land. It has been cultivated and should be included in the school land. Someone should be at work upon it, cultivating it. If it could be purchased for any reasonable sum, I would not object to securing the place as a home for myself, if it was thought advisable to do so. No time should be lost in cultivating the land. {13MR 352.2}

In the dream you have heard me relate, words were spoken of land which I was looking at, and after deep ploughing and thorough cultivating, it brought forth a bountiful harvest. {13MR 352.3}

Having had this matter presented to me at different times, I am more than ever convinced that this is the right location for the school. Since I have been here for a few days and have an opportunity to investigate, I feel more sure than at my first visit that this is the right place. I think any land which I have seen will produce some kind of crop. {13MR 352.4}

We cannot expect to find Eden, the garden of God, in this sin-desecrated earth. There will always be something to mar the most desirable place; but we do see in this land, if not faultless, a favorable place for the location of our school. These grounds will furnish the very best of gymnasiums for our young men, and for our teachers as well. Those who educate the youth in book knowledge need physical exercise to strengthen the muscles as much as do our students. Our teachers need to educate far more from nature than they do. Nature is God's great school, and on these grounds resources are found for acquiring greater knowledge of the wonderful works of God. Advantages procured by locating in this place are not presented to the teachers in such abundance in other places. {13MR 352.5}

Here is God's great farm. My mind is filled with awe as I look at these giant trees, and consider the fact that this is God's great forest garden which His own hand has planted and cared for, in promoting the growth of trees, shrubs, and beautiful ferns. God's own work is seen in the streams of water on either side of the land purchased for the school. {13MR 353.1}

On these clear, deep waters both men and women may exercise their muscles in working the oar. The youth who have been accustomed to do nothing but amuse themselves and spend money on their holidays, may here find plenty of good work in rowing boats to transport wood from the country to the cities. From the smooth waters of the river they may row into the beautiful waters of the lake, which are smooth as glass. {13MR 353.2}

I felt my heart bound with gratitude when I considered that in the providence of God the land was in our possession. The climate has marked advantages over the climate of Victoria, and I long to shout the high praises of God for so favorable a situation. John, the greatest prophet that has ever been delegated to bear a startling message to the world, obtained his education in the wilderness. The scenery of nature was before him as an open book, and God was his teacher. The flattering temptations that come to those who are crowded in the cities did not reach John in the wilderness. His eyes rested upon scenes that were pure and natural, and revealed the character of God to his soul, so that he looked up from nature to nature's God. {13MR 353.3}

Although these lands are secluded, yet they are perfectly accessible, possessing rare advantages for exporting and importing all that is necessary. Newcastle is within 20 miles, and Sydney is reached by traveling two and three quarters hours on the cars.-- Manuscript 35, 1894. {13MR 354.1}

May 1, 1894

The clearing of the land does not appear to be as formidable a task as we supposed. Some spaces are already cleared, some spaces have nothing on them but charred underbrush, with a few large monarchs of the forest still standing. There are trees of smaller growth which are as straight as an arrow. I cannot for a moment entertain the idea that land which can produce such large trees can be of a poor quality. I am sure that were the pains taken with this land, as is customary to take with land in Michigan, it would be in every way as productive. If the people in this country would take the same pains in cultivating as in America, they would be able to grow as excellent fruit, grains, and vegetables as are raised there. If they would put forth the same effort, they might take the wild land in hand, and plough and sow it with grass seed for grazing cattle. {8MR 135.1}

In May, five members of the committee visited Dora Creek and Cooranbong, and examined the tract of land which was afterward purchased for $4,500. This tract contained 1,450 acres of wild land, about 500 acres of which was thought to be suitable for the cultivation of grains, fruits, and vegetables, and for pasture. After its purchase, the estate was named "Avondale," because of the numerous creeks and the abundance of flowing water. The place chosen for school buildings is about three miles west from the Dora Creek railway station, and one and a quarter miles southeast of the Cooranbong post office. {LS 356.2}

September 2, 1894

Those who move in faith can move forward. I am ready to strike my tent at any time. The time we ought to be improving in putting in crops into the land purchased by the school, is passing away, and because of this delay we shall be left a year behind. If this is after God's order, then a mist is over my eyes, and I cannot work in courage and hope. I send this letter to you. You and others have congratulated us on the securing of land for our school; but it is not yet an assured thing that the school will be located at Dora Creek. There is some hesitancy on the part of the committee in taking up the land for this purchase! {8MR 142.3}

I shall do as I wrote you. I promised to take the school ground as my property, and I will not consider it a hard matter. I think no better missionary work could be done than to settle poor families on the land. Every family shall sign a contract that they will work the land according to the plans specified. Someone must be appointed to direct the working of the land, and under his supervision orange trees, and fruit trees of every appropriate description should be planted. Peach orchards would yield quick return. Vegetable gardens would bring forth good crops. This must be done at once. We have some six weeks yet to set things in running order, and with God's blessing on the land, we shall see what it will produce. {8MR 143.2}

The question was asked of Moses, Can the Lord spread a table in the wilderness? The question may be asked, Will this land at Dora Creek produce as abundantly as Sister White believers that it will? Time will tell. We must test the matter before we can speak assuredly, but we are willing to risk much, provided we can place the supervision of this enterprise under an understanding America farmer. We do want to demonstrate what can be done with the land when it is properly worked. When once this is done, we shall be able to help the poor who live in Australia in a far better way than by giving them money as we have had to do in the past. {8MR 143.3}

I lay out this matter before you, that you may understand the situation, and be able to advise us in regard to leaving here for Africa. We shall have to enter into the plan suggested in order to know what can be done with the Dora Creek land; for great ignorance prevails in this country as to how to make the most of the land. The Dora Creek land produces the best oranges we have tasted since coming to Australia.--Letter 29, 1894, pp. 4-8. (To S. N. Haskell, September 2, 1894.) {8MR 144.1}

November 19, 1894

Fathers and mothers, will you let your children go into all the amusements of the world? The enemy will surround them with attractions that in the end will afford no satisfaction; they will bring only weariness, disappointment, and sorrow. Will you place their hands in the hands of the world? Will you teach them to dress after its fashions, to pattern after its customs, or will you educate them to know God, and Jesus Christ whom He has sent? Shall Christ have died in vain for your children? {BEcho, November 19, 1894 par. 5}

Is there not enough in nature to reveal God's love, and draw our hearts to Him? Look at the lofty trees; look at the spires of grass that clothe our earth with its green velvet carpet; look at the flowers which our God has provided because He is a lover of the beautiful. {BEcho, November 19, 1894 par. 6}

When I was in Colorado some years since, I visited an art gallery, and there were groups of people standing before the pictures as if entranced, and praising the human artist. At evening as I was walking through the town, I saw the glory of the sunset. The bright beams were shining upon the snowcapped mountains, and it seemed as if the portals of heaven were opened, and its glory were streaming through. Persons were continually passing along the street, but none looked at the sight. My companion and myself were gazing upon it in rapture. I could discern in it heaven's beauty; I could see heaven's glory shining from the gates ajar, that we might conceive the beauty of what was within. But the crowds did not look upon the scene.

That is the way God is treated. {BEcho, November 19, 1894 par. 7}

How many go out into the garden with their children, and as they point them to the beautiful flowers say, "This is an expression of the love of God to you"? This would lead their minds up through nature to nature's God. Would not this be far more profitable to your children than taking them to all the shows and amusements of a demoralizing nature that would absorb their attention so that they forget God? {BEcho, November 19, 1894 par. 8}

April 22, 1895

I have written largely in reference to students spending an unreasonably long time in gaining an education; but I hope I shall not be misunderstood in regard to what is essential education. I do not mean that a superficial work should be done as is illustrated by the way in which some portions of the land are worked in Australia. The plow was only put in the depth of a few inches, the ground was not prepared for the seed, and the harvest was meager, corresponding to the superficial preparation that was given to the land. {SpTEd 222.1}

May 30, 1895

In God's dealings, in temporal as well as spiritual things, blessings come to man through the use of means. If the husbandman neglects to till his ground, God works no miracle to make up for his neglect; and when the harvest time comes, he has no crops to gather. As in the natural world, so in the spiritual; God always honors the use of the means he has ordained to do his work. It is by practise that men must be qualified for any emergency that may arise. Men need to become better acquainted with themselves and be discerning in regard to their own weak points of character, and then make every effort to strengthen these points, for God makes this their duty. {PC 403.1}

August 27, 1895

In the school that is started here in Cooranbong, we look to see real success in agricultural lines, combined with a study of the sciences. We mean for this place to be a center, from which shall irradiate light, precious advanced knowledge that shall result in the working of unimproved lands, so that hills and valleys shall blossom like the rose. For both children and men, labor combined with mental taxation will give the right kind of all-round education. The cultivation of the mind will bring tact and fresh incentives to the cultivation of the soil. {SpTA04 19.1}

There will be a new presentation of men as breadwinners, possessing educated, trained ability to work the soil to advantage. Their minds will not be overtaxed and strained to the uttermost with the study of the sciences. Such men will break down the foolish sentiments that have prevailed in regard to manual labor. An influence will go forth, not in loud-voiced oratory, but in real inculcation of ideas. We shall see farmers who are not coarse and rough and slack, careless of their apparel and of the appearance of their homes; but they will bring taste into farmhouses. Rooms will be sunny and inviting. We shall not see blackened ceilings, covered with cloth full of dust and dirt. Science, genius, intelligence, will be manifest in the home. The cultivation of the soil will be regarded as elevating and ennobling. Pure, practical religion will be manifested in treating the earth as God's treasure-house. The more intelligent a man becomes, the more should religious influence be radiating from him. And the Lord would have us treat the earth as a precious treasure, lent us in trust. {SpTA04 19.2}

August 27, 1895

Well, the school [Avondale College] has made an excellent beginning. The students are learning how to plant trees, strawberries, etc.; how they must keep every sprangle and fiber of the roots uncramped to give them a chance to grow. Is not this a most precious lesson as to how to treat the human mind, and the body as well, not to cramp any of the organs of the body, but give them ample room to do their work? The mind must be called out, its energies taxed. {11MR 183.1}

We want men and women who can be energized by the Spirit of God to do a complete work under the Spirit's guidance. But these minds must be cultivated, employed to do thorough work, not lazy and dwarfed by inaction. Just so men and women and children are wanted who will work the land, and use their tact and skill, not with a feeling that they are menials, but that they are doing just such noble work as God gave to Adam and Eve in Eden, who love to see the miracles wrought by the Divine Husbandman. The human agent plants the seed and God waters it, and causes His sun to shine upon it, and up springs the tiny blade. Here is the lesson God gives to us concerning the resurrection of the body and the renewing of the heart. We are to learn of spiritual things from the development of the earthly. . . . {11MR 183.2}

The spiritual lessons to be learned are of no mean order. The seeds of truth sown in the soil of the heart will not all be lost, but will spring up, first the blade, then the ear, then the full corn in the ear. God said in the beginning, "Let the earth bring forth grass, the herb yielding seed, and the fruit tree yielding fruit." God created the seed as He did the earth, by the divine word. We are to exercise our reasoning power in the cultivation of the earth, and to have faith in the word of God that has created the fruit of the earth for the service of man. {11MR 184.1}

The cultivation of our land requires the exercise of all the brain power and tact we possess. The unworked lands around us testify to the indolence of men. We hope to arouse to action the dormant senses. We hope to see intelligent farmers, who will be rewarded for their earnest labor. The hand and head must cooperate, bringing new and sensible plans into operation in the cultivation of the soil. We have here seen the giant trees felled and uprooted, we have seen the ploughshare pressed into the earth, turning deep furrows for the planting of trees and the sowing of the seed. The students are learning what ploughing means, and that the hoe and the shovel and the rake and the harrow are all implements of honorable and profitable industry. Mistakes will often be made, but every error lies close beside truth. Wisdom will be learned by failures, and the energy that will make a beginning gives hope of success in the end. . . . {11MR 184.2}

For both children and men, labor combined with mental taxation will give the right kind of all-round education. The cultivation of the mind will bring tact and fresh incentive to the cultivation of the soil. {11MR 184.3}

The more intelligent a man becomes, the more religious influence should be radiating from him. And the Lord would have us treat the earth as a precious treasure, lent us in trust.--Letter 47a, 1895, pp. 5-8. (To J. H. Kellogg, August 27, 1895.) {11MR 184.4}

August 28, 1895

Large tracts of beautiful land lie uncleared, unworked. The timber business has brought the settlers a meager pittance, and almost every day we see a drove of bullocks used to draw one, or sometimes two or three large logs. We count six, seven, or eight span, moving slowly along with their burden. Six span of bullocks were used to plow our land for cultivation. They are under discipline, and will move at a word and a crack of a whip, which makes a sharp report, but does not touch them. They wheel into line when it seems that they must get tangled up, but the creatures understand their business, and they plod patiently with the immense plow used to break up the unworked soil. {8MR 93.2}

The people about here have raised no vegetables, and but little fruit, except a few oranges and lemons that are not cultivated, and I have seen a few peach trees. Land is profitless, but in the land boom it cost eight pounds an acre, some of which now sells for four. Thousands of acres lie untouched; for no one attempts to work the land. They think it will yield nothing, but we know it will yield if properly cultivated. {8MR 93.3}

The school land, fifteen hundred acres, was purchased for $5,500. The school has twelve acres put into orchard, I have two acres in fruit trees. We shall experiment on this land, and if we make a success, others will follow our example. Notwithstanding oranges and lemons have yielded year after year, not a new tree is planted by the settlers. Their indolence and laziness causes false witness to be borne against the land. When right methods of cultivation are adopted there will be far less poverty than now exists. {8MR 94.1}

I did not expect to write you in this way, but these particulars we want you to have that you may understand what we are doing. We intend to give the people practical lessons upon the improvement of the land, and thus induce them to cultivate their land, now lying idle. If we accomplish this, we shall have done good missionary work. {8MR 94.2}

Today Mr. Moseley comes to bring oranges and lemon trees for us to set out. As soon as this work is done, we shall begin to plant vegetables. We have to get our groceries from Sydney, nearly a hundred miles away, or from Newcastle, twenty-two miles. But we hope soon to raise our own fruit and vegetables. Willie cannot be here, so I am here in his place, where I can oversee matters, and plan and consult with the workmen. I am called out from my routine of writing, yet I arise at half past one, at two, and three o'clock, and for a week have done considerable writing.--Letter 42, 1895, pp. 1-4. (To J. H. Kellogg, August 28, 1895.) {8MR 94.3}

November 26, 1895

Why should not Seventh-day Adventists become true laborers together with God in seeking to save the souls of the colored race? Instead of a few, why should not many go forth to labor in this long-neglected field? Where are the families who will become missionaries and who will engage in labor in this field? Where are the men who have means and experience so that they can go forth to these people and work for them just where they are? There are men who can educate them in agricultural lines, who can teach the colored people to sow seed and plant orchards. There are others who can teach them to read, and can give them an object lesson from their own life and example. Show them what you yourself can do to gain a livelihood, and it will be an education to them. Are we not called upon to do this very work? Are there not many who need to learn to love God supremely and their fellow men as themselves? In the Southern field are many thousands of people who have souls to save or to lose. Are there not many among those who claim to believe the truth who will go forth into this field to do the work for which Christ gave up His ease, His riches, and His life? {RH, November 26, 1895 par. 5}

1896 – Oakwood Industrial School Founded

May 11, 1896

In choosing retired localities for our schools, we do not for a moment suppose that we are placing the youth beyond the reach of temptation. Satan is a very diligent worker, and is untiring in devising ways to corrupt every mind that is open to his suggestions. He meets families and individuals on their own ground, adapting his temptations to their inclinations and weaknesses. But in the large cities his power over minds is greater, and his nets for the entanglement of unwary feet are more numerous. In connection with our schools, ample grounds should be provided. There are some students who have never learned to economize, and have always spent every shilling they could get. These should not be cut off from the means of gaining an education. Employment should be furnished them, and with their study of books should be mingled a training in industrious, frugal habits. Let them learn to appreciate the necessity of helping themselves. {SpTEd 45.2}

There should be work for all students, whether they are able to pay their way or not; the physical and mental powers should receive proportionate attention. Students should learn to cultivate the land; for this will bring them into close contact with nature. {SpTEd 46.1}

There is a refining, subduing influence in nature that should be taken into account in selecting the locality for a school. God has regarded this principle in training men for his work. Moses spent forty years in the wilds of Midian. John the Baptist was not fitted for his high calling as the forerunner of Christ by association with the great men of the nation in the schools at Jerusalem. He went out into the wilderness, where the customs and doctrines of men could not mold his mind, and where he could hold unobstructed communion with God. {SpTEd 46.2}

God would have us appreciate his blessings in his created works. How many children there are in the crowded cities that have not even a spot of green grass to set their feet upon. If they could be educated in the country, amid the beauty, peace, and purity of nature, it would seem to them the spot nearest heaven. In retired places, where we are farthest from the corrupting maxims, customs, and excitements of the world, and nearest to the heart of nature, Christ makes his presence real to us, and speaks to our souls of his peace and love. {SpTEd 46.4}

May 20, 1896

While the Bible should hold the first place in the education of children and youth, the book of nature is next in importance. God's created works testify to his love and power. He has called the world into being, with all that it contains. God is a lover of the beautiful; and in the world which he has fitted up for us, he has not only given us everything necessary for our comfort, but he has filled the heavens and the earth with beauty. We see his love and care in the rich fields of autumn, and his smile in the glad sunshine. His hand has made the castle-like rocks and the towering mountains. The lofty trees grow at his command; he has spread earth's green velvet carpet, and dotted it with shrubs and flowers. Why has he clothed the earth and trees with living green, instead of a dark, somber brown? Is it not that they may be more pleasing to the eye? And shall not our hearts be filled with gratitude, as we read the evidences of his wisdom and love in the wonders of his creation? {SpTEd 58.1}

The same creative energy that brought the world into existence is still exerted in upholding the universe and continuing the operations of nature. The hand of God guides the planets in their orderly march through the heavens. It is not because of inherent power that year by year the earth continues her motion round the sun, and produces her bounties. The word of God controls the elements. He covers the heavens with clouds, and prepares rain for the earth. He makes the valley fruitful, and "grass to grow upon the mountains." It is through his power that vegetation flourishes; that the leaves appear, and the flowers bloom. {SpTEd 58.2}

The whole natural world is designed to be an interpreter of the things of God. To Adam and Eve in their Eden home, nature was full of the knowledge of God, teeming with divine instruction. It was vocal with the voice of wisdom to their attentive ears. Wisdom spoke to the eye, and was received into the heart; for they communed with God in his created works. As soon as the holy pair transgressed the law of the Most High, the brightness from the face of God departed from the face of nature. Nature is now marred and defiled by sin. But God's object-lessons are not obliterated; even now, rightly studied and interpreted, she speaks of her Creator. {SpTEd 59.1}

As divine truth is revealed in Holy Writ, so it is reflected, as from a mirror, in the face of nature; and through his creation we become acquainted with the Creator. And so the book of nature becomes a great lesson book, which instructors who are wise can use, in connection with the Scriptures, to guide lost sheep back to the fold of God. As the works of God are studied, the Holy Spirit flashes conviction into the mind. It is not the conviction which logical reasoning produces; but unless the mind has become too dark to know God, the eye too dim to see him, the ear too dull to hear his voice, a deeper meaning is grasped, and the sublime, spiritual truths of the written word are impressed on the heart. {SpTEd 59.2}

The most effective way to teach the heathen who know not God, is through his works. In this way, far more readily than by any other method, they can be made to realize the difference between their idols, the works of their own hands, and the true God, the Maker of heaven and earth. The same principle applies to the ignorant, neglected colored race in that part of America where slavery once existed. When these lowly members of the human family have learned to know God through his works, a foundation will be laid for the spiritual truths of the written word, which will elevate and purify their characters. {SpTEd 59.3}

There is a simplicity and purity in these lessons directly from nature that make them of the highest value to others besides the heathen. The children and youth, all classes of students, need the lessons to be derived from this source. In itself the beauty of nature leads the soul away from sin and worldly attractions, and toward purity, peace, and God. For this reason the cultivation of the soil is good work for children and youth. It brings them into direct contact with nature and nature's God. And that they may have this advantage in connection with our schools there should be, as far as possible, large flower gardens and extensive lands for cultivation. {SpTEd 60.1}

An education amid such surroundings is in accordance with the directions which God has given for the instruction of youth; but it is in direct contrast with the methods employed in the majority of schools. Parents and teachers have disregarded the counsel of the Lord. Instead of following the light he has given, they have walked in the sparks of their own kindling. The minds of the young have been occupied with books of science and philosophy, where the thorns of skepticism have been only partially concealed; with vague, fanciful fairy stories; or with the works of authors, who, although they may write on Scripture subjects, weave in their own fanciful interpretations. The teaching of such books is as seed sown in the heart. It grows and bears fruit, and a plentiful harvest of infidelity is reaped; and the result is seen in the depravity of the human family. {SpTEd 60.2}

A return to simpler methods will be appreciated by the children and youth. Work in the garden and field will be an agreeable change from the wearisome routine of abstract lessons, to which their young minds should never be confined. To the nervous child, who finds lessons from books exhausting and hard to remember, it will be especially valuable. There is health and happiness for him in the study of nature; and the impressions made will not fade out of his mind, for they will be associated with objects that are continually before his eyes. {SpTEd 61.1}

God has, in the natural world, placed in the hands of the children of men the key to unlock the treasure-house of his word. The unseen is illustrated by the seen; divine wisdom, eternal truth, infinite grace, are understood by the things that God has made. Then let the children and youth become acquainted with nature and nature's laws. Let the mind be developed to the utmost capacity, and the physical powers trained for the practical duties of life; but teach them also that God has made this world fair because he delights in our happiness; and that a more beautiful home is preparing for us in that world where there will be no more sin. The word of God declares, "Eye hath not seen, nor ear heard, neither have entered into the heart of man, the things which God hath prepared for them that love him." {SpTEd 61.2}

The little children should come especially close to nature. Instead of putting fashion's shackles upon them, let them be free like the lambs, to play in the sweet, fresh sunlight. Point them to shrubs and flowers, the lowly grass and the lofty trees, and let them become familiar with their beautiful, varied, and delicate forms. Teach them to see the wisdom and love of God in his created works; and as their hearts swell with joy and grateful love, let them join the birds in their songs of praise. {SpTEd 62.1}

Educate the children and youth to consider the works of the great Master Artist, and to imitate the attractive graces of nature in their character building. As the love of God wins their hearts, let them weave into their lives the beauty of holiness. So shall they use their capabilities to bless others and honor God. {SpTEd 62.2}

August 13, 1896

Education means more than the mere studying of books. It is necessary that both the physical and mental powers be exercised in order to have a proper education. When in counsel with the Father before the world was, it was designed that the Lord God should plant a garden for Adam and Eve in Eden, and give them the task of caring for the fruit trees, and cultivating and training the vegetation. Useful labor was to be their safeguard, and it was to be perpetuated through all generations to the close of earth's history. To have a whole-sided education, it is necessary to combine science with practical labor. From infancy children should be trained to do those things that are appropriate for their age and ability. Parents should now encourage their children to become more independent. Serious troubles are soon to be seen upon the earth, and children should be trained in such a way as to be able to meet them. Many parents give a great deal of time and attention to amusing their children, encouraging them to bring all their troubles to them; but children should be trained to amuse themselves, to exercise their minds in devising plans for their own satisfaction, doing the simple things that are natural for them to do. {ST, August 13, 1896 par. 5}

Fathers should train their sons to engage with them in their trades and employments. Farmers should not think that agriculture is a business that is not elevated enough for their sons. Agriculture should be advanced by scientific knowledge. Farming has been pronounced unprofitable. People say that the soil does not pay for the labor expended upon it, and they bemoan the hard fate of those who till the soil. In this country (Australia) many have given up the idea that the land will pay for working it, and thousands of acres lie unimproved. But should persons of proper ability take hold of this line of employment, and make a study of the soil, and learn how to plant, to cultivate, and to gather in the harvest, more encouraging results might be seen. Many say, "We have tried agriculture, and know what its results are," and yet these very ones need to know how to cultivate the soil, and to bring science into their work. Their plowshares should cut deeper, broader furrows, and they need to learn that in tilling the soil they need not become common and coarse in their natures. Let them learn to bring religion into their work. Let them learn to put in the seed in its season, to give attention to vegetation, and to follow the plan that God has devised. {ST, August 13, 1896 par. 8}

The farmer and his sons have the open book of nature before them, and they should learn that farming is a noble occupation, when the work is done in a proper manner. The opinion that prevails that farming degrades the man, is erroneous. The earth is God's own creation, and he calls it very good. The hands may become hard and rough, but this hardness need not extend to the soul. The heart need not become careless, nor the soul defiled. The effeminate paleness may be tanned from the countenance, but the testimony of health is seen in the red and brown of the complexion. Christlikeness may be preserved in the farmer's life. Men may learn, in cultivating the soil, precious lessons about the cultivation of the Spirit. {ST, August 13, 1896 par. 9}

Note: These are the last two paragraphs in an article on parents disciplining their children.

December 8, 1896

God gives to us, that we may give. He desires us to be laborers together with him. In heaven he is carrying forward the great work of redemption. That work engages the divine councils. It requires the ministry of angels upon the earth; and it requires also our co-operation. In the natural world, man must do his part in the work of the earth. He must till and prepare the soil. And God, working through nature, giving sunshine and showers, quickens the seed sown, and causes vegetation to flourish. Thus the sowing is rewarded in the reaping of earth's treasures in bountiful harvests. The lesson is true in spiritual as in temporal things. Man must work under the guidance of the divine hand; for unless God co-operates with him, there will be no increase. Human power cannot cause the seed sown to spring into life. But there can be no reaping unless the human hand acts its part in the sowing of the seed. {RH, December 8, 1896 par. 6}

December 16, 1896 (Written from Australia)

I determined to set my trees, even before the foundation of the house was built. We broke up only furrows, leaving large spaces unplowed. Here in these furrows we planted our trees the last of September, and lo, this year they were loaded with beautiful blossoms and the trees were loaded with fruit. It was thought best to pick off the fruit, although the trees had obtained a growth that seemed almost incredible. The small amount of fruit--peaches and nectarines--have served me these three weeks. They were delicious, early peaches. We have later peaches--only a few left to mature as samples. Our pomegranates looked beautiful in full bloom. Apricots were trimmed back in April and June, but they threw up their branches and in five weeks, by measurement, had a thrifty growth of five and eight feet. {8MR 252.2}

If the Lord prospers us next year, as He has done the past year, we will have all the fruit we wish to take care of, early and late. The early fruit comes when there is nothing else, so this is an important item. The peaches are rich and juicy and grateful to the taste. We have quince trees set out, and lemon, orange, apple, plum, and persimmon trees. We have even planted elderberry bushes. We planted our vineyard in June. Everything is flourishing and we shall have many clusters of grapes this season. {8MR 252.3}

We have a large strawberry bed which will yield fruit next season. We have a few cherry trees, but the testimony is that the land is not good for cherries. But so many false, discouraging testimonies have been borne in regard to the land that we pay no attention to what they say. We shall try every kind of a tree. We have a large number of mulberry trees and fig trees of different kinds. This is not only good fruit land, but it is excellent in producing root crops and tomatoes, beans, peas, potatoes--two crops a season. All these good treasures that the land will yield have been brought in from Sydney and Newcastle and thousands of acres of land have been untouched because the owners say they will not raise anything. We have our farm as an object lesson. {8MR 252.4}

The school orchard is doing excellently well. If the land is worked it will yield its treasures, but weeds will grow and those who own land will not exercise ambition to take these weeds out by the roots and give them no quarter. Deep plowing must be done. They let a few orange trees grow in the sod, also the lemons. We get the choicest, best oranges for three pence and two pence ha'penny [half penny] per dozen--six cents American money, and four and five cents per dozen for large, beautiful, sweet oranges. {8MR 253.1}

We have a large space of land devoted to ornamental trees and flowers. I have scoured the country for different plants and I have a large bush of lemon verbena honeysuckle. We have a large variety of roses, dahlias, gladioli, geraniums, pinks, pansies, and evergreens.

This must be a sample settlement, to tell what can be raised here.-- Letter 162, 1896, pp. 2, 3. (To J. E. White, December 16, 1896.) {8MR 253.2}

December 20, 1896

In every school Satan will try to make himself the guide of the teachers who are instructing the students. It is he who would introduce the idea that selfish amusements are a necessity. It is he who would lead students, sent to our schools for the purpose of receiving an education and training for the work of evangelists, ministers, and missionaries, to believe that amusements are essential to keep them in physical health, when the Lord has presented to them that the better way is for them to embrace manual labor in their education, and thus let useful employment take the place of selfish amusements. These amusements, if followed, soon develop a dislike for useful, healthful exercise of body and mind, such as would make students efficient to serve themselves and others. {8MR 151.3}

The education to be gained in the felling of trees, the tilling of the soil, and the erection of buildings, as well as the studies of the classroom, is what our youth should seek to obtain. Tent making also should be taught, buildings should be erected, and masonry should be learned. Further on, a printing press should be connected with the school, that an education may be given to students in this line of work. {8MR 152.1}

There are many things which the women students may also engage in, such as cooking, dressmaking, and gardening. Plants and flowers should be cultivated, strawberries should be planted. Thus the women students may be called out of doors to gain healthful exercise, and to be educated in useful labor. Book binding also, and a variety of trades should be taken up. These will not only give exercise to brain, bone, and muscle, but they will also give knowledge of great value. The greatest curse of our world today is idleness. The students coming to our school have had an abundance of amusements, which serve merely to please and gratify self. They are now to be given a different education, that they may be prepared to go forth from the school prepared for any service. {8MR 152.2}

The proper cooking of foods is a most important accomplishment. Especially where meat is not made a principal article of food, is good cooking an essential requirement. Something must be prepared to take the place of meat, and these substitutes for meat must be well prepared, so that meat will not be desired. {8MR 153.1}

Education and culture on all points of practical experience will fit our youth for usefulness when they shall leave school to engage in mission work at home or in foreign countries. They will not then be dependent upon the people to whom they go to cook for them, to sew for them, or to build their habitations. Rather, they will be prepared to educate the ignorant to show others how to do all manner of labor by plans and methods that will produce the best results, and they will thus become much more influential and helpful. {8MR 153.2}

Their abilities will be especially appreciated where money is hard to obtain, for a much smaller fund will be required to sustain such missionaries. Those who have put to the very best use their physical powers in useful, practical labor, while obtaining an education, will show that missionaries can become successful teachers and educators in various lines of labor, and, wherever they go, all that they have gained in these lines will give them favor, influence, and power. {8MR 153.3}

It is also very essential that students shall understand the principles of medical missionary work, for, wherever students may be called, they need a knowledge of the science of how to treat the sick. This will give them a welcome anywhere, because there is suffering of every kind in every part of the world. {8MR 153.4}

It is an important matter that students be given an education that will fit them for successful business life. In many schools, the education given is one-sided. In our school the common branches should be fully and thoroughly taught. Bookkeeping is one of the most important lines of study to fit students for practical business life. Bookkeeping should be looked upon as of equal importance with grammar. And yet, there are very few who leave our schools with a clear knowledge of how to correctly keep accounts. Those who have a living interest in the cause and work of God should never allow themselves to settle down with the idea that they are not required to know how to keep accounts. {8MR 154.1}

The reason for many of the mistakes made in accounts and the failure in business matters is because men have not a thorough knowledge of bookkeeping. They are not prompt in making a faithful record of all transactions and keeping a daily account of their expenditures, and many are charged with being dishonest, when they were not designedly dishonest. Their failure was come through a lack of knowledge of accounts. Many a youth, because of ignorance in the matter of keeping accounts, has been led into errors that have caused him serious trouble. {8MR 154.2}

True education means much. We have no time now to spend in speculative ideas, or in haphazard movements. The evidences that the coming of Christ is near are many and are very plain, and yet many who profess to be looking for Him are asleep. We are not half as earnest as we ought to be to gather up the important truths that are for our admonition, upon whom the ends of the world are come. Unless we understand the importance of passing events, and make ready to stand in the great day of God, we shall be registered in the books of heaven as unfaithful stewards. The watchman is to know the time of the night. Everything is now clothed with a solemnity that all who believe the truth should feel and understand. They should act in reference to the great day of God. {8MR 154.3}

Our time is precious. We have but few days left of probation, in which to qualify ourselves for the future eternal life. We are not to devote these precious moments to cheap, common, or superficial things. We shall have to guard against the holding of ideas and maxims which may be presented as essential from a human standpoint, for it is not the words of worldly wisdom, it is not the maxims of men, or the theories of human beings that will qualify us for acceptable service. Rather, it is the word of the living God. In all our schools this word is to be made the essence of education. It is in feeding upon the word of God that we obtain the divine element that the soul needs in order to secure a healthy development of all its spiritual powers. Those who dig deep for the hidden treasure will find their reward in the precious veins of ore, and these hidden truths will make them wise unto salvation. They are following the example of their Saviour, and all the wiles and subtilties of Satanic agencies cannot beguile them from a position of steadfast self-denial.--Letter 60a, 1896, pp. 1-6. (To "The Friends of the [Avondale] School," December 20, 1896.) {8MR 155.1}

1897 – Avondale College Founded

June 9, 1897

We have begun to clear our land here in the woods. One year ago last August Mrs. May White, Ella and Mabel White, and myself kindled the first brush fire, beginning to clear the land. It was very interesting work for the children; they enjoyed it ever so much. Four tents were then pitched, and the men began the work of felling trees, and preparing the land for cultivation. A breaking up plough, drawn by sixteen oxen broke up the land. The land was simply ploughed. We could not then afford to do more than this. . . . {7MR 252.3}

In this way we employed men who had worked at the cabinet maker's trade, carriage builders, and painters. They were in poverty and great need, and some had large families to provide for. We paid them not less than a dollar a day, and fed them. In this way we have worked to get a few acres cleared and planted in peaches, apricots, plums, pears, nectarines, apples, figs, oranges, and lemons. These trees were planted in the furrows the last of September and the first of October. The next April the entire orchard was ploughed again. By the next August, the trees were fragrant with blossoms. In November there was beautiful fruit on the peach and nectarine trees. These trees had been loaded with fruit, but most of it had been picked off when small. It was thought best for the trees to do this. With the blessing of God, by the coming November we shall have plenty of fruit. {7MR 253.1}

Our school is located here. Their land was cleared and planted with trees at the same time that my orchard was planted. This coming season we expect that it will bear fruit for the school. Our people are settling in this place. Here students are to be educated in books, and are also to be taught how to do all kinds of manual labor. The Lord will help us in this work. This is the first term of school. There are sixty students in attendance. Thirty of these come from a distance, and live in the home. All the students are young men and young women of excellent capabilities. {7MR 253.2}

We have located [Avondale] here on missionary soil, and we design to teach the people all round us how to cultivate the land. They are all poor because they have left their land uncultivated. We are experimenting, and showing them what can be done in fruit raising and gardening. {7MR 253.3}

For the benefit of our school we knew that we must get away from the cities, where there are so many holidays, and where the interest taken in ball playing, horse racing, and games of every kind, amounts almost to a craze. In the woods we are just where we should be. Not that we expect to get away from Satan and from temptation, but we do hope to be able to teach the youth that there is something satisfying besides amusement. {7MR 254.1}

August 15, 1897

The school [Avondale College] was established at a great expense, both of time and labor, to enable students to obtain an all-round education, that they might gain a knowledge of agriculture, a knowledge of the common branches of education, and above all, a knowledge of the Word of God.... {11MR 173.3}

The proportionate taxation of the powers of mind and body will prevent the tendency to impure thoughts and actions. Teachers should understand this. They should teach students that pure thoughts and actions are dependent on the way in which they conduct their studies. Conscientious actions are dependent on conscientious thinking. Exercise in agricultural pursuits and in the various branches of labor is a wonderful safeguard against undue brain taxation. No man, woman, or child who fails to use all the powers God has given him can retain his health. He cannot conscientiously keep the commandments of God. He cannot love God supremely and his neighbor as himself.... {11MR 174.1}

Health and a clear conscience will attend those who work faithfully, keeping the glory of God in view. There are many who are mere fragments of men. In Christ is seen the perfection of Christian character. He is our pattern. His life was not a life of indolence or ease. He lived not to please Himself. He was the Son of the infinite God, yet He worked at the carpenter's trade, with His father. As a member of the home firm, He faithfully acted His part in helping to support the family.... {11MR 174.2}

Men, women, and children should be educated to labor with their hands. Then the brain will not be overtaxed to the detriment of the whole organism.... {11MR 174.3}

Completeness of Christian character is possible. How? "Ye are complete in Him" (Colossians 2:10).--Letter 145, 1897, pp. 3, 6, 9, 10. (To W. C. White, August 15, 1897.) {11MR 174.4}

August 18, 1897

When the power invested in kings is allied to goodness, it is because the one in responsibility is under the divine dictation. When power is allied with wickedness, it is allied to Satanic agencies, and it will work to destroy those who are the Lord's property. The Protestant world have set up an idol sabbath in the place where God's Sabbath should be, and they are treading in the footsteps of the Papacy. For this reason I see the necessity of the people of God moving out of the cities into retired country [places,] where they may cultivate the land and raise their own produce. Thus they may bring their children up with simple, healthful habits. I see the necessity of making haste to get all things ready for the crisis. Letter 90, 1897. {12MR 219.4}

> Note: This paragraph is taken from a letter written to Brother and Sister Lindsay. The context of the letter is entirely eschatological and no other comments are made about farming.

September 2, 1897

A man's success in the ministry does not rest upon his excluding himself from useful labor, nor upon his popularity or indolence, but upon his willingness to labor in any position that seems to be duty. Those who are the most willing to toil and show industry in business lines, and who, themselves, plan and devise to be a help to others in branches of common toil, are the men who will be chosen by God to do Him service wherever their lot may be cast. They may be called upon with the help of others to build their own homes, or to build a church, or to do this alone, if they have a knowledge of how to handle tools. {19MR 26.1}

Privation may be the lot of every soul who now believes and obeys the truth. Christ has told us that we will have reproach. If persecution for the truth's sake is to come, it is important that every line of work become familiar to us, that we and our families may not suffer through lack of knowledge. We can and should have tact and knowledge in trades, in building, in planting, and in sowing. A knowledge of how to cultivate the land will make rough places much smoother. This knowledge will be counted a great blessing, even by our enemies. {19MR 26.2}

September 24, 1897

"Ye are God's husbandry." Will the students apply this lesson while they are working upon the land, tilling the soil, plowing and harrowing, putting all the skill they possess into the work of bringing the land into a condition where it will be fit for the planting of the seed, and the trees, preparatory for the harvest? Will they bear in mind that they are God's husbandry, a part of the Lord's farm, and that in this term of school there is a great deal of work to be done by those who are appointed to watch for souls as they that must give an account? There are hearts that need much more labor bestowed upon them because the soil has not been under the plow or the harrow. The hardened soil must be broken up and subdued, so that the Word of God, the gospel seed, may find favorable soil for the production of a harvest. {11MR 37.1}

Let the students call all their faculties of discernment to bear upon this subject. Let their skills interpret the figures used. The earth has to be worked to bring out its varied properties favorable to the growth of the seed and fruit. But the harvest will reward the painstaking efforts made in a supply of food for the necessities of man.... {11MR 37.2}

There must be an intelligent, harmonious cooperation of the divine and human. The working of the soil is a lesson book, which if read will be of the greatest benefit to every student in our school. They may understand that surface work, haphazard half-effort, will reveal itself in the harvest to be garnered.... {11MR 37.3}

1898

The question asked during the Saviour's ministry, "How knoweth this man letters, having never learned?" does not indicate that Jesus was unable to read, but merely that He had not received a rabbinical education. John 7:15. Since He gained knowledge as we may do, His intimate acquaintance with the Scriptures shows how diligently His early years were given to the study of God's word. And spread out before Him was the great library of God's created works.

He who had made all things studied the lessons which His own hand had written in earth and sea and sky. Apart from the unholy ways of the world, He gathered stores of scientific knowledge from nature. He studied the life of plants and animals, and the life of man. From His earliest years He was possessed of one purpose; He lived to bless others. For this He found resources in nature; new ideas of ways and means flashed into His mind as He studied plant life and animal life. Continually He was seeking to draw from things seen illustrations by which to present the living oracles of God. The parables by which, during His ministry, He loved to teach His lessons of truth show how open His spirit was to the influences of nature, and how He had gathered the spiritual teaching from the surroundings of His daily life. {DA 70.2}

Thus to Jesus the significance of the word and the works of God was unfolded, as He was trying to understand the reason of things. Heavenly beings were His attendants, and the culture of holy thoughts and communings was His. From the first dawning of intelligence He was constantly growing in spiritual grace and knowledge of truth. {DA 70.3} Every child may gain knowledge as Jesus did. As we try to become acquainted with our heavenly Father through His word, angels will draw near, our minds will be strengthened, our characters will be elevated and refined. We shall become more like our Saviour. And as we behold the beautiful and grand in nature, our affections go out after God. While the spirit is awed, the soul is invigorated by coming in contact with the Infinite through His works. Communion with God through prayer develops the mental and moral faculties, and the spiritual powers strengthen as we cultivate thoughts upon spiritual things. {DA 70.4}

March, 1898

He [God] employs many unseen agencies to make the seeds apparently thrown away, living plants. First appear the blade, then the ear, then the full corn in the ear. God creates the electricity that gives life to the seed, vitality to the blade, the ear, and the corn in the ear. Who else can be depended on to give the due proportion required of all the agencies to perfect the harvest of fruits and grains? Let man employ his agencies to the utmost limit; he must then depend on his Creator, who knows just what is needed for the harvest, which is connected to Him by wonderful links of His own wonderful power, beyond the human agency. Without these unseen agencies, seed is valueless.--Ms 34, 1898. {3MR 322.1}

Note: Manuscript 25 was typed up on Feb. 24, 1898 and Manuscript 37 on Mar. 11, 1898.

April 14, 1898

We would do well to consider the case of Elisha when chosen for his work. The prophet Elijah was about to close his earthly labors. Another was to be called to carry forward the work for that time. In his course of travel, Elijah was directed northward. How changed the scene before him now from that which the country had presented a little while before. Then the farming districts were unworked; the ground was parched; for neither dew nor rain had fallen for three years. Now everything seems to be springing up as if to redeem the time of famine and dearth. The plenteous rains had done more for the earth than for the hearts of humanity; the fields were better prepared for labor than were the hearts of apostate Israel. {YI, April 14, 1898 par. 4}

Wherever Elijah looked, the land he saw was owned by one man,--a man who had not bowed the knee to Baal, whose heart had remained undivided in the service of God. Even during the captivity there were souls who had not gone into apostasy, and this family was included in the seven thousand who had not bowed the knee to Baal. The owner of the land was Shaphat. Busy activity was seen among the workers. While the flocks were enjoying the green pastures, the busy hands of his servants were sowing the seed for a harvest. {YI, April 14, 1898 par. 5}

The attention of Elijah was attracted to Elisha, the son of Shaphat, who with the servants was plowing with twelve yoke of oxen. He was educator, director, and worker. Elisha did not live in the thickly populated cities. His father was a tiller of the soil, a farmer. Far from city and court dissipation, Elisha had received his education. He had been trained in habits of simplicity, of obedience to his parents and to God. Thus in quietude and contentment he was prepared to do the humble work of cultivating the soil. But though of a meek and quiet spirit, Elisha had no changeable character.

Integrity and fidelity and the love and fear of God were his. He had the characteristics of a ruler, but with it all was the meekness of one who would serve. His mind had been exercised in the little things, to be faithful in whatsoever he should do; so that if God should call him to act more directly for him, he would be prepared to hear his voice. {YI, April 14, 1898 par. 6}

The surroundings of Elisha's home were those of wealth; but he realized that in order to obtain an all-round education, he must be a constant worker in any work that needed to be done. He had not consented to be in any respect less informed than his father's servants. He had learned how to serve first, that he might know how to lead, instruct, and command. {YI, April 14, 1898 par. 7}

Elisha waited contentedly, doing his work with fidelity. Day by day, through practical obedience and the divine grace in which he trusted, he obtained rectitude and strength of purpose. While doing all that he possibly could in co-operating with his father in the home firm, he was doing God's service. He was learning how to co-operate with God. {YI, April 14, 1898 par. 8}

The youth should bear in mind that their physical strength, their mental qualifications, and their spiritual endowments, are to be devoted to service. These are never to be misapplied, never misused, never left to rust through inaction. Elisha increased in knowledge daily. Daily he prepared to do service in any way that opened before him. He served God in the little temporal duties. He grew in knowledge and in grace. And if the student today will develop reliability and soundness of principle in the things which are least, he will reveal that he has acquired adaptability to serve God in a higher capacity. He who feels that it is of no great consequence to serve in the lesser capacity will never be trusted of God to serve in the more honored position. He may present himself as fully competent to accomplish the duties of the higher position; but God looks deeper than the surface. A watcher is on his track, and after test and trial, there is written against him, "Thou art weighed in the balances, and art found wanting." That sentence in the courts of heaven decides for eternity the destiny of the human being. {YI, April 14, 1898 par. 9}

June 14, 1898

As they cultivate the soil, the students are to learn spiritual lessons. The plow must break up the fallow ground. It must lie under the rays of the sun and the purifying air. Then the seed, to all appearance dead, is to be dropped into the prepared soil. Trees are to be planted, seeds for vegetables sown. And after man has acted his part, God's miracle-working power gives life and vitality to the things placed in the soil. In this agricultural process, there are lessons to be learned. Man is not to do slothful work. He is to act the part appointed him by God. His industry is essential if he would have a harvest.--Ms. 71, 1898, p. 2. ("Come Up to the Help of the Lord," June 14, 1898.) {11MR 177.4}

June 26, 1898

Before I visited Cooranbong, the Lord gave me a dream. In my dream I was taken to the land that was for sale in Cooranbong. Several of our brethren had been solicited to visit the land, and I dreamed that I was walking upon the ground. I came to a neat-cut furrow that had been plowed one quarter of a yard deep and two yards in length. Two of the brethren who had been acquainted with the rich soil of Iowa were standing before this furrow and saying, "This is not good land; the soil is not favorable." But One who has often spoken in counsel was present also, and He said, "False witness has been borne of this land." Then He described the properties of the different layers of earth. He explained the science of the soil, and said that this land was adapted to the growth of fruit and vegetables, and that if well worked it would produce its treasures for the benefit of man. This dream I related to Brother and Sister Starr and my family. {16MR 153.1}

The next day we were on the cars, on our way to meet others who were investigating the land; and as I was afterward walking on the ground where the trees had been removed, lo, there was a furrow just as I had described it, and the men also who had criticized the appearance of the land. The words were spoken just as I had dreamed. {16MR 153.2}

August 26, 1898

As we are about to establish our facilities for the manufacture of health foods, the question has come up: How shall we treat this matter? Where shall we locate the work so important to ourselves and to the school established in Cooranbong? Shall this branch of business be established in Cooranbong, and thus open ways and means whereby many more students may obtain an all-round education? {SpM 134.3}

From the light given me in regard to the location and building up of our school interests, I know that it is the purpose of God that this institution be established at a distance from the city that is so full of temptations and snares, of amusements and holidays, which are not conducive to purity and piety and religious devotion. He designs that we shall connect manual labor with the improvement of the mental powers. I have been shown that study in agricultural lines should be the A B and C of the educational work of our schools. This institution must not depend upon imported produce,--for the fruits so essential to healthfulness, and for their grains and vegetables. This is the very first work that must be entered upon. Then as we shall advance and add to our facilities, advance studies and object lessons should come in. We are not to subtract from that which has already been taken hold of as a branch of education. {SpM 134.4}

All the arts are to come into the education of the students. Even in the school at Avondale there are too many studies taken by the students. The youth should not be left to take all the studies they shall choose, for they will be inclined to take more than they can carry; and if they do this, they cannot possibly come from the school with a thorough knowledge of each study. There should be less study of books, and greater painstaking effort made to obtain that knowledge which is essential for practical life. The youth are to learn how to work interestedly and intelligently, that, wherever they are, they may be respected because they have a knowledge of those arts which are so essential for practical life. In the place of being day laborers under an overseer, they are to strive to be masters of their trades to place themselves where they can command wages as good carpenters, printers, or as educators in agricultural work. Ms 105, 1898, pp. 2,3. ("The Education Our School Should Give," August 26, 1898.) {SpM 135.3}

September 14, 1898

Last Friday night after retiring, a great burden came upon me. I could not sleep until midnight. About the time of the beginning of the Sabbath, I lay down upon the lounge, and (an unusual thing for me to do) fell asleep. Then some things were presented before me. {8MR 264.1}

Some persons were selecting allotments of land, on which they purposed to build their homes, and One stood in our midst and said, "You are making a great mistake which you will have cause to regret. This land is not to be occupied with buildings except to provide the facilities essential for the teachers and students of the school. This is the school farm. This land is to be reserved as an acted parable to the students. They are not to look upon the school land as a common thing, but as a lesson book which the Lord would have them study. Its lessons will impart knowledge in the spiritual culture of the soul. {8MR 264.2}

"For you to settle this land with private houses, and then be driven to select other land at a distance for school purposes would be a great mistake, always to be regretted. All the land upon the ground that is not needed for buildings is to be considered the school farm, where youth may be educated under well-qualified superintendents.". . . {8MR 264.3}

The Lord would have the school grounds dedicated to Him as His own school room. The church premises are not to be invaded with houses. We are located where there is plenty of land. . . . {8MR 264.4}

"Thus saith the Lord, the heaven is my throne, and the earth is my footstool: where is the house that ye build unto me? and where is the place of my rest? For all those things hath mine hand made, and all those things have been, saith the Lord: but to this man will I look, even to him that is poor and of a contrite spirit, and trembleth at my word." (Isaiah 66:1.) {8MR 265.1}

We have had an experience to teach us what this means. Nearly one year ago, as we were living the last days of the old year, my heart was in a burdened condition. I had matters opening before me in regard to the dangers of disposing of land near the school for dwelling houses. We seemed to be in a council meeting, and there stood One in our midst who was expected to help us out of our difficulties. The words spoken were plain and decided, "This land, by the appointment of God, is for the benefit of the school. You have recently had an evidence of human nature, what it will reveal under temptation. The more families you settle about the school buildings, the more difficult it will be for teachers and students.--Ms 115, 1898, pp. 1, 3, 6. ("The School Farm," September 14, 1898.) {8MR 265.2}

September 16, 1898

The educational advantages of our school are to be of a distinct order. This school farm is God's lesson book. Those who till the soil and plant and cultivate the orchard are to make the application of nature's lessons, and bring these lessons learned into their actual spiritual experience. Let every individual bear in mind that "whatsoever a man soweth, that shall he also reap." The man who day by day sows objectionable seeds, in words, in deportment, in spirit, is conforming himself to the same character, and this is determining the future harvest he will reap. Then let ministers and their wives, let the teachers of the youth in any line, close the door to jealousy and evil surmising of those whom God uses to do His work. {18MR 2.2}

Holiness, which means wholeness to God, is wholly acceptable to God. A Paul may plant, and Apollos water, but God giveth the increase. "He that soweth to his flesh, shall of the flesh reap corruption; but he that soweth to the Spirit, shall of the Spirit reap life everlasting" [Galatians 6:8]. As the workers till the soil, they are to reap all the advantages possible by making an application of the lessons they receive. In the natural world unseen agencies are constantly at work to produce the essential results, but the harvest to be reaped depends upon the seed that has been sown. After man faithfully prepares the land, and plants the seed, God must work constantly to cause the seed to germinate. {18MR 6.2}

So it is in spiritual things. The word of the living God is the seed, Christ is the sower, and unless He constantly works the soil of the heart, there will be no harvest. "Ye are God's husbandry; ye are God's building." God gave His Son to die, the Just for the unjust, that there might be a glorious harvest of souls. The human heart is God's seed plot, and the righteousness of Christ must be cherished there. Then let no man trust in the arm of flesh, but in God. Let each give evidence that he has faith, that he is not a religious dwarf, but that he grows under the dews and showers of the grace of Christ, that his life of righteousness is not of man's creating, but that it is the righteousness of Christ, which the grace of God has nourished in his heart. {18MR 7.1}

Note: These quotes are taken from Ms. 116, ("Two Great Principles of the Law," Sept. 16, 1898.) and were written as an illustration of spiritual truth. They are the only paragraph on farming in the manuscript.

September 24, 1898

You say, You have not answered my question [THE QUESTION WAS: "WHAT SHALL WE DO WITH THE [OLD] SCHOOL BUILDING? SHALL WE SELL IT TO THE SANITARIUM? SHALL WE ESTABLISH SCHOOLS IN DIFFERENT LOCALITIES?"--LETTER 75, 1898, P. 1.] yet. I would say, The same reasons that have led us to move away from the city and locate our school here [Avondale, Australia], stand good with you in America. The money that is expended in buildings, when they are thousands of dollars in debt, is not in God's order. In this you are not following the path that God has marked out. The counsel of God has not been regarded. Had the money which has been expended in adding to the college building been invested in procuring land in connection with the school, you would not have so large a number of students, with their debts increasing, in the city of Battle Creek. {8MR 199.1}

Let the students be out in the most healthful location that can be secured, to do the very work that should have been done years ago. Then there would not be so great discouragements. Had this been done, you would have had some grumbling from students, and many objections would have been raised by parents, but this all-round education would educate the children and youth, not only for practical work in various trades, but would prepare them for the Lord's farm in the earth made new. If all in America had encouraged the work in agricultural lines that principals and teachers have discouraged, the schools would have had altogether a different showing. Opposing influences would have been overcome; circumstances would have changed; there would have been greater physical and mental strength; labor would have been equalized; and the taxing of all the human machinery would have proved the sum. But the directions God has been pleased to give you, you have taken hold of so gingerly, that you have not had the ability to overcome obstacles. It reveals cowardice to move as slowly and uncertainly as you have done in the labor line, for this is the very best kind of education that can be obtained. {8MR 199.2}

Opposing circumstances will and should create a firm determination to overcome them. One barrier broken down will give greater ability and courage to go forward. Fate has not woven its meshes about the workings of our schools that they need to remain helpless and in uncertainty. Press in the right direction, and make a change, solidly, intelligently. Then circumstances will be your helpers and not your hindrances. {8MR 200.1}

Nature is our lesson book. "Ye are God's husbandry, ye are God's building" (1 Corinthians 3:9.) The Lord has not laid out His lines that you should be in uncertainty. The building up of so much that is in Battle Creek the Lord will surely counterwork, if His voice is not heeded, by bringing around circumstances that will pull them down. {8MR 200.2}

Look at nature. There is room in her vast boundaries for schools to be located where grounds can be cleared, land cultivated, and where a proper education can be given. This work is essential for an all-round education, and one which is favorable to spiritual advancement. Nature's voice is the voice of Jesus Christ teaching us innumerable lessons of perseverance. The mountains and hills are changing, the earth is waxing old like a garment, but the blessing of God, which spreads a table for His people in the wilderness, will never cease. {8MR 200.3}

Serious times are before us, and there is great need for the families to get out of the cities into the country, that the truth may be carried into the highways and byways of the earth. Much depends upon your laying your plans according to the word of the Lord, and with persevering energies to go ahead. More depends upon active perseverance than upon genius and book knowledge. All the talents and ability given to human agents, if unworked, are of no value. The talent of genius must be constantly worked. Make a beginning. The tree is in the acorn, and the acorn in the tree. {8MR 200.4}

There are those who are not adapted to agricultural work. These should not devise and plan in our conferences, for they will hold everything from advancing in these lines. This has held our people from advancing in the past. If the land is cultivated, it will with the blessing of God, supply our necessities.--Letter 75, 1898, pp. 6, 7. (To E. A. Sutherland, September 24, 1898.) {8MR 201.1}

October 5, 1898

Plans were laid to build cottages on the school campus [Avondale College]. I was glad I was here at the time that this subject was brought up, for I had something to say. I told them that the grounds were not to be occupied by buildings. The land is to be our lesson book. After being cleared, it is to be cultivated. Orange, lemon, peach, apricot, nectarine, plum, and apple trees are to occupy the land, with vegetable gardens, flower gardens, and ornamental trees. Thus this place is to be brought as near as possible to the presentation that passed before me several times, as the symbol of what our school and premises should be. Dwelling houses, fenced allotments for families were not to be near our school buildings. This place must by the appointment of God be a representation of what school premises should be--a delight to the eyes. {11MR 185.3}

The open book of nature is to be the student's study. Schools should be established away from the cities. I have more invested in this land than any other person. I am carrying students through school, paying their expenses that they may get a start. This gives me an influence with teachers and learners. The land was laid out in lots. Houses were to be built, as in a village. But I tell them that buildings are not to be crowded upon the land around the school buildings. This is God's farm, and it is sacred ground. Here the students are to learn the lesson, "Ye are God's husbandry; ye are God's building." The work that is done in the land is to be done in a particular, thorough, wise manner. From the cultivation of the soil and the planting of seed, lessons in spiritual lines may be learned. {11MR 186.1}

All kinds of industrial employment are to be found for the student. The students are constantly to learn how to use brain, bone, and muscle, taxing all harmoniously and equally.--Letter 84, 1898, pp. 8, 9. (To J. H. Kellogg, October 5, 1898.) {11MR 186.2}

October 11, 1898

Mr. H. C. Thompson, our farmer, then presented some of the products of the soil. Oranges and lemons from our school orchard, sweet potatoes and other products from the garden, were shown with pride; for they were all of extraordinary size and quality. He spoke briefly of what may be realized as the result of a faithful cultivation of the land, and pointed out that some of the difficulties that must be encountered by the agriculturist in this climate are largely compensated for by the fact that we can successfully engage in the cultivation of garden crops all the year around. {RH, October 11, 1898 par. 16}

The meeting closed with an earnest appeal from the chairman for the people of Cooranbong and vicinity to unite in the development of the district by the planting of orchards and the cultivation of garden produce, so that all may live upon the products of the soil, and not have to subsist on the bodies of dead animals. {RH, October 11, 1898 par. 17}

The good influence of this meeting was felt throughout the week of prayer; and the spirit of cordial friendship continues to grow. {RH, October 11, 1898 par. 18}

Note: These paragraphs describe a presentation that was given by the farmer at Avondale during a week of prayer held in Cooranbong during the last week of May in 1898.

February 1, 1899

Our schools must be conducted under the supervision of God. There is a work to be done for young men and young women that is not yet accomplished. There are much larger numbers of young people who need to have the advantages of our school. They need the manual-training course, which will teach them how to lead an active, energetic life. All kinds of labor must be connected with our school. Under wise, judicious, God-fearing directors, the students are to be taught. Every branch of the work is to be conducted on the most thorough and systematic lines that long experience and wisdom can plan and execute. {Advocate, February 1, 1899 par. 1}

Let the teachers in our school wake up, and impart the knowledge they have in agricultural lines, and in the industries that it is essential for the students to understand,--seek in every line of labor to reach the very best results. Let the science of the word of God be brought into the work, that the students may understand correct principles, and may reach the highest possible standard. Exert your God-given abilities, and bring all your energies into the development of the Lord's farm. Study and labor, that the best results and the greatest returns may come from the seed sowing, that there may be an abundant supply of food, both temporal and spiritual. {Advocate, February 1, 1899 par. 2}

The Work before Us.--We need more teachers and more talent, to educate the students in various lines, that there may go forth from this place many persons willing and able to carry the knowledge which they have received to others. Lads are to come in from different localities, and nearly all will take the industrial course. This course should include the keeping of accounts, carpenter's work, and everything that is comprehended in farming. Preparation should also be made for the teaching of blacksmithing, painting, shoemaking, cooking, baking, washing, mending, typewriting, and printing. Every power at our command is to be brought into this training work, that students may go forth equipped for the duties of practical life. {Advocate, February 1, 1899 par. 3}

Cottages and buildings essential to the school work are to be erected by the students themselves. These buildings should not be crowded close together, or located near the school buildings proper. In the management of this work, small companies should be formed who should be taught to carry a full sense of their responsibility. All these things can not be accomplished at once, but we are to begin to work in faith. {Advocate, February 1, 1899 par. 4}

March 11, 1899

I have been broken off to have a talk with Brother Martin. I furnish him with papers and tracts to do missionary work. He is not a minister, but a farmer of considerable intelligence. He sells fruit, and thus becomes acquainted with the people. Many souls have been converted through his zealous influence. I have just told him he needed the Review and Herald, and that he must take it. He put his hand in the pocket and handed me the money. I am going to send in all the names I can get; for every family ought to have our church paper. Please send the Review to F. Martin, Kellyville, New South Wales, Australia, and charge the same to my account. {PH079 6.1}

April 25, 1899

Christ never planted the seeds of death in the system. Satan planted these seeds when he tempted Adam to eat of the tree of knowledge, which meant disobedience to God. Not one noxious plant was placed in the Lord's great garden, but after Adam and Eve sinned, poisonous herbs sprang up. In the parable of the sower the question was asked the master, "Didst not thou sow good seed in thy field? From whence then hath it tares?" The master answered, "An enemy hath done this." [Matthew 13:27, 28.] All tares are sown by the evil one. Every noxious herb is of his sowing, and by his ingenious methods of amalgamation he has corrupted the earth with tares. {16MR 247.2}

July 11, 1899

Many children are left to come up with less attention from their parents than a good farmer devotes to his dumb animals. Fathers, especially, are often guilty of manifesting less care for wife and children than that shown to their cattle. A merciful farmer will take time to devote especial thought as to the best manner of managing his stock, and will be particular that his valuable horses shall not be overworked, overfed, or fed when heated, lest they be ruined. He will take time to care for his stock, lest they be injured by neglect, exposure, or any improper treatment, and his increasing young stock depreciate in value. He will observe regular periods for their eating, and will know the amount of work they can perform without injuring them. In order to accomplish this, he will provide them only the most healthful food, in proper quantities, and at stated periods. By thus following the dictates of reason, farmers are successful in preserving the strength of their beasts. If the interest of every father, for his wife and children, corresponded to that care manifested for his cattle, in that degree that their lives are more valuable than the dumb animals, there would be an entire reformation in every family, and human misery be far less. {RH, July 11, 1899 par. 4}

Great care should be manifested by parents in providing the most healthful articles of food for themselves and for their children.

And in no case should they place before their children food which their reason teaches them is not conducive to health, but which would fever the system, and derange the digestive organs. Parents do not study from cause to effect in regard to their children, as in the case of their dumb animals, and do not reason that to overwork, to eat after violent exercise and when much exhausted and heated, will injure the health of human beings, as well as the health of dumb animals, and will lay the foundation for a broken constitution in man, as well as in the beasts. {RH, July 11, 1899 par. 5}

July 31, 1899

On several occasions the light has come to me that Avondale is to be used as the Lord's farm. In a special sense there is to be connected with this farm land that shall be highly cultivated. Spread out before me there was land planted with every kind of fruit trees that will bear fruit in this locality, also vegetable gardens, where seeds were sown and cultivated. {AUCR, July 31, 1899 par. 10}

If the managers of this farm and the teachers in the school will receive the Holy Spirit to work with them, they will have wisdom in their management, and God will bless their labours. The planting and the sowing, the gathering of the harvest, and the care of the trees, are to be wonderful lessons for all the students. The invisible links which connect the sowing and the reaping are to be studied, and the goodness of God is to be pointed out and appreciated. It is the Lord that gives the virtue and the power to the soil and to the seed. Were it not for His divine agency, combined with human tact and ability, the seed sown would be useless. There is an unseen power constantly at work as man's servant, to feed and to clothe him. The parable of the seed as studied in the daily experience of teacher and student is to reveal that God is at work in nature, and it is to make plain the things of the kingdom of heaven. {AUCR, July 31, 1899 par. 11}

Next to the Bible, nature is to be our great lesson book. But there is no virtue in deifying nature, for this is exalting the thing made above the great Master Artist who designed the work, and who keeps it every hour operating according to His appointment. As we plant the seed, and cultivate the plant, we are to remember that God created the seed, and He gives it to the earth. By His divine power

He cares for that seed. It is by His appointment that the seed in dying gives its life to the blade, which contains in itself other seeds to be treasured and again put into the earth to yield their harvest. We may also study how the co-operation of man acts a part. The human agent has his part to act, his work to do. This is one of the lessons which nature teaches, and we shall see in it a solemn, a beautiful work. {AUCR, July 31, 1899 par. 12}

There is much talk about the Lord in nature, as if God were bound by the laws of nature to be nature's servant. In this men do not know what they are talking about. Do they suppose that nature has a self-existing power without the continual agency of Jehovah? Many theories would lead minds to suppose that nature was a self-sustaining agency apart from Deity, having its own inherent power with which to work. The Lord does not exert His laws to supersede the laws of nature. He does His work through the laws and the properties of His instruments, and nature obeys a "Thus saith the Lord." {AUCR, July 31, 1899 par. 13}

The God of nature is perpetually at work. His infinite power works unseen, but manifestations appear in the effects which the work produces. The same God who guides the planets works in the fruit orchard and in the vegetable garden. He never made a thorn, a thistle, or a tare. These are Satan's work, the result of degeneration, introduced by him among the precious things; but it is through God's immediate agency that every bud bursts into blossom. When He was in the world in the form of humanity, Christ said: "My Father worketh hitherto, and I work." John 5:17. So when the students employ their time and strength in agricultural work, in heaven it is said of them, Ye "are laborers together with God." 1 Corinthians 3:9. {AUCR, July 31, 1899 par. 14}

Let the lands near the school and the church be retained. Those who come to settle in Cooranbong can, if they choose, find for themselves homes near by, or on portions of, the Avondale Estate. But the light given to me is that all that section of land from the school orchard to the Maitland road, and extending on both-sides of the road from the meeting house to the school, should become a farm and a park, beautified with fragrant flowers and ornamental trees. There should be fruit orchards and every kind of produce cultivated that is adapted to this soil, that this place may become an object lesson to those living close by and afar off. {AUCR, July 31, 1899 par. 15}

Then let everything not essential to the work of the school be kept at a distance, and thus prevent any disturbance of the sacredness of the place through the proximity of families and buildings. Let the school stand alone. There must not be this one and that one claiming personal property near it. It will be better for private families, however devoted they may be in the service of the Lord, to be located at some distance from the school buildings. The school is the Lord's property, and the grounds about it are His farm, where the great Sower can make His garden a lesson book. The results of the labours will be seen, "first the blade, then the ear, then the full corn in the ear." The land will yield its treasures, bringing the joyousness of an abundant harvest, and the produce gathered through the blessing of God is to be used as nature's lesson book from which spiritual lessons can be made plain, and applied to the necessities of the soul. {AUCR, July 31, 1899 par. 16}

August, 1899

The Lord has given His life to the trees and vines of His creation. His word can increase or decrease the fruit of the land. If men would open their understanding to discern the relation between nature and nature's God, faithful acknowledgments of the Creator's power would be heard. Without the life of God, nature would die. His creative works are dependent on Him. He bestows life-giving properties on all that nature produces. We are to regard the trees laden with fruit as the gift of God, just as much as though He placed the fruit in our hands (MS 114, 1899). {1BC 1081.4}

August 24, 1899

The tithing system was instituted by the Lord as the very best arrangement to help the people in carrying out the principles of the law. If this law were obeyed, the people would be entrusted with the entire vineyard, the whole earth. "Wherefore ye shall do my statutes, and keep my judgments, and do them; and ye shall dwell in the land in safety. And the land shall yield her fruit, and ye shall eat your fill, and dwell therein in safety. And if ye shall say, What shall we eat the seventh year? behold, we shall not sow, nor gather in our increase: Then I will command my blessing upon you in the sixth year, and it shall bring forth fruit for three years. And ye shall sow the eighth year, and eat yet of old fruit until the ninth year; until her fruits come in ye shall eat of the old store".... {1BC 1112.5}

Men were to cooperate with God in restoring the diseased land to health, that it might be a praise and a glory to His name. And as the land they possessed would, if managed with skill and earnestness, produce its treasures, so their hearts, if controlled by God, would reflect His character.... {1BC 1112.6}

In the laws which God gave for the cultivation of the soil, He was giving the people opportunity to overcome their selfishness and become heavenly-minded. Canaan would be to them as Eden if they obeyed the Word of the Lord. Through them the Lord designed to teach all the nations of the world how to cultivate the soil so that it would yield healthy fruit, free from disease. The earth is the Lord's vineyard, and is to be treated according to His plan. Those who cultivated the soil were to realize that they were doing God service. They were as truly in their lot and place as were the men appointed to minister in the priesthood and in work connected with the tabernacle. God told the people that the Levites were a gift to them, and no matter what their trade, they were to help to support them.   MS 121, 1899 {1BC 1112.7}

Note: The paragraphs above only appears in the SDA Bible Commentary and the devotional Be Like Jesus, meaning that the MS in its entirety has not yet been released. As a consequence, I do not know the actual writing of the full MS. However, MS 120, 1899 was written on Aug. 23, 1899, and MS 123, 1899 was written on Aug. 25, 1899.

August 24, 1899

The seventh year after they [Israel] settled in Canaan was to be a Sabbath year. All agricultural business was to stop. There was to be no planting or sowing. For one year the people were to depend wholly on the Lord, having faith in His arrangements as the householder. The land needed a rest in order to renew the forces necessary for growth. That which grew of itself was the common property of the poor and the stranger, the cattle and the herds. Thus the land was to receive rest, and the poor and the cattle a feast. {3MR 347.2}

This was to show that nature was not God, that God controlled nature. God designed that from nature His church should constantly learn important lessons. They were to cherish a vivid sense that God was the manager, the householder. They were to know the reality of His presence and His providential care over all the earth. They were to realize that all nature was under His supervision, all the productions of the ground under His ministration. This was to give them faith in His providence. He could withhold His blessings or bestow them.--Ms 121, 1899. {3MR 347.3}

August, 1899

I have things to send to you in writing that I deem very important, and I think it will be prepared in a form so that many may be benefited by it. I should oft be so pleased to have talks with you upon matters that are intensely interesting to me, that I am trying to write out in reference to the specifications in scriptural injunctions in regard to the duties one to another in Leviticus and Deuteronomy. We must just call to our minds those [precepts on] actual, practical missionary work, and work intelligently, and do the very principles of Christianity, the gospel of the Old Testament. {13MR 135.2}

And this some call the Dark Ages. If so, it is not because they had no communication from heaven. Leviticus 25. The Lord was over the whole earth. Every seventh year was a sabbatical year. This would be a wonderful arrangement down in this age of great light. Not only the agricultural processes were to be intermitted, but the cultivation of the soil was not permitted. It lay in its spontaneous growth for the benefit of the poor. All had free access to it--the strangers and the flocks and herds. This was to invigorate the productive, worn-out soil, and to teach the Hebrew nation that God was the Householder, and the people were His tenants. The land had a sabbath, or yearly sabbath. {13MR 135.3}

Then the jubilee, the fiftieth. The lessons given were to encourage liberality and overcome all stinginess, and to give lessons to all that it was the Lord's land. He was to be regarded as its owner, that He would make it productive, if they were obedient, by giving them His blessing upon their lands. The lesson given was that the Lord was taking care of the poor, and that He had made provision for them; and every seventh year the spontaneous crops were for them. This is the principle of liberality; a provision was made by special interposition of God. The sixth year, under God's supervision, the land yielded provision for three years; and it was a constant lesson that God was the Householder, and the land was His. {13MR 136.1}

January 1, 1900

We must open to our students the Book of all books, the living oracles of God. Here true wisdom is to be found. In all matters that pertain to our present duty to God, and to our future, eternal interests, we may here receive divine instruction. And we are to learn from nature. We thank the Lord that we are located just where we are. The land we are cultivating as the school farm is testifying to all that false witness has been borne against it. We are making this land an educating book for the students. From it they are to learn the meaning of the words, "We are labourers together with God; ye are God's husbandry; ye are God's building." {AUCR, January 1, 1900 par. 13}

January 31, 1900

Our brethren have selected a site for our new sanitarium. It is about thirteen miles from Sydney, and is in an excellent, healthful location. The altitude is about six hundred feet, and the place receives the cool, life-giving breeze from the sea. Thus, while in the low-lying towns the atmosphere is impure, hot, and oppressive, here it is pure, cool, and refreshing. Excellent roads, and beautiful, picturesque scenery afford opportunity for pleasant drives. Freedom from the dust and the smoke, the din and the confusion, of the city will be most grateful to the brain-weary and the sick. {11MR 221.1}

It was not God's purpose that people should be crowded into cities, huddled together in terraces and tenements. In the beginning He placed our first parents in a garden, amidst the beautiful sights and sounds of nature, and these sights and sounds He desires men to rejoice in today. The more nearly we can come into harmony with God's original plan, the more favorable will be our position for the recovery and preservation of health. {11MR 221.2}

Our retired location will offer comparative freedom from many of the temptations of city life. Here are no liquor-selling hotels or dram-shops on every corner to tempt the unfortunate victim of intemperance. And the pure sights and sounds, the clear, invigorating air, and the sense of God's presence pervading all nature, tend to uplift the mind, to soften the heart, and to strengthen the will to resist temptation. {11MR 221.3}

While affording the benefits of country life, our sanitarium will be sufficiently near Sydney to secure the advantages of connection with the city. There are two railway lines leading into Sydney. The stations are about twenty minutes' drive from the sanitarium farm, and trains run almost hourly into the city. Five or six little villages within a few miles of our site are fast filling up with the residences of businessmen from the city. This district seems destined to be the most desirable of all the suburbs of Sydney. Not a person who has seen our location of land has one word of criticism to offer. All are surprised that we have purchased it so cheaply. We are sure that it possesses advantages above any other place we have seen. {11MR 222.1}

1900

The parable of the seed reveals that God is at work in nature. The seed has in itself a germinating principle, a principle that God Himself has implanted; yet if left to itself the seed would have no power to spring up. Man has his part to act in promoting the growth of the grain. He must prepare and enrich the soil and cast in the seed. He must till the fields. But there is a point beyond which he can accomplish nothing. No strength or wisdom of man can bring forth from the seed the living plant. Let man put forth his efforts to the utmost limit, he must still depend upon One who has connected the sowing and the reaping by wonderful links of His own omnipotent power. {COL 63.1}

There is life in the seed, there is power in the soil; but unless an infinite power is exercised day and night, the seed will yield no returns. The showers of rain must be sent to give moisture to the thirsty fields, the sun must impart heat, electricity must be conveyed to the buried seed. The life which the Creator has implanted, He alone can call forth. Every seed grows, every plant develops, by the power of God. {COL 63.2}

Such are a few of the many lessons taught by nature's living parable of the sower and the seed. As parents and teachers try to teach these lessons, the work should be made practical. Let the children themselves prepare the soil and sow the seed. As they work, the parent or teacher can explain the garden of the heart with the good or bad seed sown there, and that as the garden must be prepared for the natural seed, so the heart must be prepared for the seed of truth. As the seed is cast into the ground, they can teach the lesson of Christ's death; and as the blade springs up, they can teach the lesson of the truth of the resurrection. As the plants grow, the correspondence between the natural and the spiritual sowing may be continued. {COL 87.2}

The youth should be instructed in a similar way. They should be taught to till the soil. It would be well if there were, connected with every school, lands for cultivation. Such lands should be regarded as God's own schoolroom. The things of nature should be looked upon as a lesson book which His children are to study, and from which they may obtain knowledge as to the culture of the soul. {COL 87.3} In tilling the soil, in disciplining and subduing the land, lessons may constantly be learned. No one would think of settling upon a raw piece of land, expecting it at once to yield a harvest. Earnestness, diligence, and persevering labor are to be put forth in treating the soil preparatory to sowing the seed. So it is in the spiritual work in the human heart. Those who would be benefited by the tilling of the soil must go forth with the word of God in their hearts. They will then find the fallow ground of the heart broken by the softening, subduing influence of the Holy Spirit. Unless hard work is bestowed on the soil, it will not yield a harvest. So with the soil of the heart: the Spirit of God must work upon it to refine and discipline it before it can bring forth fruit to the glory of God. {COL 88.1}

The soil will not produce its riches when worked by impulse. It needs thoughtful, daily attention. It must be plowed often and deep, with a view to keeping out the weeds that take nourishment from the good seed planted. Thus those who plow and sow prepare for the harvest. None need stand in the field amid the sad wreck of their hopes. {COL 88.2}

The blessing of the Lord will rest upon those who thus work the land, learning spiritual lessons from nature. In cultivating the soil the worker knows little what treasures will open up before him. While he is not to despise the instruction he may gather from minds that have had an experience, and from the information that intelligent men may impart, he should gather lessons for himself. This is a part of his training. The cultivation of the soil will prove an education to the soul. {COL 88.3}

He who causes the seed to spring up, who tends it day and night, who gives it power to develop, is the Author of our being, the King of heaven, and He exercises still greater care and interest in behalf of His children. While the human sower is planting the seed to sustain our earthly life, the Divine Sower will plant in the soul the seed that will bring forth fruit unto life everlasting. {COL 89.1}

Through disobedience to God, Adam and Eve had lost Eden, and because of sin the whole earth was cursed. But if God's people followed His instruction, their land would be restored to fertility and beauty. God Himself gave them directions in regard to the culture of the soil, and they were to co-operate with Him in its restoration. Thus the whole land, under God's control, would become an object lesson of spiritual truth. As in obedience to His natural laws the earth should produce its treasures, so in obedience to His moral law the hearts of the people were to reflect the attributes of His character. Even the heathen would recognize the superiority of those who served and worshiped the living God. {COL 289.2}

Ellen White began her 23 day voyage back from Australia on Aug. 29, 1900

1901 – Battle Creek College Moved to Berrien Springs

The Southern Years (1901-1909)

April 12, 1901 – Ellen White at the 1901 General Conference Session

The light that has been given me is that Battle Creek has not the best influence over the students in our school. There is altogether too congested a state of things. The school, although it will mean a fewer number of students, should be moved out of Battle Creek. Get an extensive tract of land, and there begin the work which I entreated should be commenced before our school was established here,--to get out of the cities, to a place where the students would not see things to remark upon and criticise, where they would not see the wayward course of this one and that one, but would settle down to diligent study. {GCB, April 14, 1901 par. 44}

Every term of school which we have held at Avondale has resulted in the conversion of nearly every student in the school. In some terms this has been the case without exception, and in others there have not been more than two or three exceptions. Business men have brought their children from Newcastle to our school in Avondale, so that they would not be tempted as they would be in the public schools, which they declared were corrupted. Our schools should be located away from the cities, on a large tract of land, so that the students will have opportunity to do manual work. They should have opportunity to learn lessons from the objects which Christ used in the inculcation of truth. He pointed to the birds, to the flowers, to the sower and the reaper. {GCB, April 14, 1901 par. 45}

In schools of this kind not only are the minds of the students benefited, but their physical powers are strengthened. All portions of the body are exercised. The education of mind and body is equalized. The body needs a great deal more care than it gets. There are men here who are suffering, O so much, because they are not faithful stewards of their bodies. God wants you to use every means in your power to care for the wonderful machinery which he has given you. Let no part of it rust from inaction. {GCB, April 14, 1901 par. 46}

When students study the popular literature of the present day, evil will be sure to crop out. When young ladies read novels, they are led away from the living experience which they should gain in the truth. Instead of preparing themselves for missionary work, they pore over novels, by which they are made just as drunk as is a drunkard by the liquor which he drinks. Thus the mind is impaired, and they are made unable to study. {GCB, April 14, 1901 par. 47}

Students should have manual work to do, and it will not hurt them if in doing this work they become weary. Do you not think Christ became weary?--Indeed he did. Weariness injures no one. It only makes rest sweeter. It will not hurt the students to deny appetite, and live on a simple diet of fruits and grains. This will help them. It will strengthen and bless them. It is a meat diet, and a great variety of food, which is ruining the digestive organs. None of our schools are to indulge in these harmful things. {GCB, April 14, 1901 par. 48}

The young men, as well as the young women are to be taught how to cook; and the young women, as well as the young men, are to take a part in outside work. When this is done, there will be found in our schools in America as healthy a class of students as is found in our school in Cooranbong, where there are few of the students whose health has not been improved by correct habits of life. {GCB, April 14, 1901 par. 49}

Note: The above paragraphs led to the move of Battle Creek College to Berrien Springs in the months following the General Conference session.

1901 (Appears original was an Advocate article of Aug. 1, 1900)

Because difficulties arise, we are not to drop the industries that have been taken hold of as branches of education. While attending school the youth should have an opportunity for learning the use of tools. Under the guidance of experienced workmen, carpenters who are apt to teach, patient, and kind, the students themselves should erect buildings on the school grounds and make needed improvements, thus by practical lessons learning how to build economically. The students should also be trained to manage all the different kinds of work connected with printing, such as typesetting, presswork, and book binding, together with tentmaking and other useful lines of work. Small fruits should be planted, and vegetables and flowers cultivated, and this work the lady students may be called out of doors to do. Thus, while exercising brain, bone, and muscle, they will also be gaining a knowledge of practical life. {6T 176.1}

Culture on all these points will make our youth useful in carrying the truth to foreign countries. They will not then have to depend upon the people among whom they are living to cook and sew and build for them, nor will it be necessary to spend money to transport men thousands of miles to plan schoolhouses, meetinghouses, and cottages. Missionaries will be much more influential among the people if they are able to teach the inexperienced how to labor according to the best methods and to produce the best results. They will thus be able to demonstrate that missionaries can become industrial educators, and this kind of instruction will be appreciated especially where means are limited. A much smaller fund will be required to sustain such missionaries, because, combined with their studies, they have put to the very best use their physical powers in practical labor; and wherever they may go all they have gained in this line will give them vantage ground. Students in the industrial departments, whether they are employed in domestic work, in cultivating the ground, or in other ways, should have time and opportunity given them to tell the practical, spiritual lessons they have learned in connection with the work. In all the practical duties of life, comparisons should be made with the teachings of nature and of the Bible. {6T 176.2}

The reasons that have led us in a few places to turn away from cities and locate our schools in the country, hold good with the schools in other places. To expend money in additional buildings when a school is already deeply in debt is not in accordance with God's plan. Had the money which our larger schools have used in expensive buildings been invested in procuring land where students could receive a proper education, so large a number of students would not now be struggling under the weight of increasing debt, and the work of these institutions would be in a more prosperous condition. Had this course been followed, there would have been some grumbling from students, and many objections would have been raised by parents; but the students would have secured an all-round education, which would have prepared them, not only for practical work in various trades, but for a place on the Lord's farm in the earth made new. {6T 177.1}

Had all our schools encouraged work in agricultural lines, they would now have an altogether different showing. There would not be so great discouragements. Opposing influences would have been overcome; financial conditions would have changed. With the students, labor would have been equalized; and as all the human machinery was proportionately taxed, greater physical and mental strength would have been developed. But the instruction which the Lord has been pleased to give has been taken hold of so feebly that obstacles have not been overcome. {6T 177.2}

It reveals cowardice to move so slowly and uncertainly in the labor line--that line which will give the very best kind of education. Look at nature. There is room within her vast boundaries for schools to be established where grounds can be cleared and land cultivated. This work is essential to the education most favorable to spiritual advancement; for nature's voice is the voice of Christ, teaching us innumerable lessons of love and power and submission and perseverance. Some do not appreciate the value of agricultural work. These should not plan for our schools, for they will hold everything from advancing in right lines. In the past their influence has been a hindrance. {6T 178.1}

If the land is cultivated, it will, with the blessing of God, supply our necessities. We are not to be discouraged about temporal things because of apparent failures, nor should we be disheartened by delay. We should work the soil cheerfully, hopefully, gratefully, believing that the earth holds in her bosom rich stores for the faithful worker to garner, stores richer than gold or silver. The niggardliness laid to her charge is false witness. With proper, intelligent cultivation the earth will yield its treasures for the benefit of man. The mountains and hills are changing; the earth is waxing old like a garment; but the blessing of God, which spreads a table for His people in the wilderness, will never cease. {6T 178.2}

Serious times are before us, and there is great need for families to get out of the cities into the country, that the truth may be carried into the byways as well as the highways of the earth. Much depends upon laying our plans according to the word of the Lord and with persevering energy carrying them out. More depends upon consecrated activity and perseverance than upon genius and book learning. All the talents and ability given to human agents, if unused, are of little value. {6T 178.3}

A return to simpler methods will be appreciated by the children and youth. Work in the garden and field will be an agreeable change from the wearisome routine of abstract lessons, to which their young minds should never be confined. To the nervous child, who finds lessons from books exhausting and hard to remember, it will be especially valuable. There is health and happiness for him in the study of nature; and the impressions made will not fade out of his mind, for they will be associated with objects that are continually before his eyes. {6T 179.1}

Working the soil is one of the best kinds of employment, calling the muscles into action and resting the mind. Study in agricultural lines should be the A, B, and C of the education given in our schools. This is the very first work that should be entered upon. Our schools should not depend upon imported produce, for grain and vegetables, and the fruits so essential to health. Our youth need an education in felling trees and tilling the soil as well as in literary lines. Different teachers should be appointed to oversee a number of students in their work and should work with them. Thus the teachers themselves will learn to carry responsibilities as burden bearers. Proper students also should in this way be educated to bear responsibilities and to be laborers together with the teachers. All should counsel together as to the very best methods of carrying on the work. {6T 179.2}

Time is too short now to accomplish that which might have been done in past generations. But even in these last days we can do much to correct the existing evils in the education of youth. And because time is short, we should be in earnest and work zealously to give the young an education consistent with our faith. We are reformers. We desire that our children should study to the best advantage. In order to do this, employment should be given them which will call into exercise the muscles. Daily, systematic labor should constitute a part of the education of youth even at this late period. Much can now be gained in this way. In following this plan the students will realize elasticity of spirit and vigor of thought, and in a given time can accomplish more mental labor than they could by study alone. And thus they can leave school with constitutions unimpaired and with strength and courage to persevere in any position where the providence of God may place them. {6T 179.3}

1901

There are some things regarding the disposition and use of the lands near our school and church which have been opened before me and which I am instructed to present to you. Until recently I have not felt at liberty to speak of them, and even now I do not feel free to reveal all things because our people are not yet prepared to understand all that in the providence of God will be developed at Avondale. {6T 181.1}

In the visions of the night some things were clearly presented before me. Persons were selecting allotments of land near the school, on which they proposed to build houses and establish homes. But One stood in our midst who said: "You are making a great mistake which you will have cause to regret. This land is not to be occupied with buildings except to provide the facilities essential for the teachers and students of the school. This land about the school is to be reserved as the school farm. It is to become a living parable to the students. The students are not to regard the school land as a common thing, but are to look upon it as a lessonbook open before them which the Lord would have them study. Its lessons will impart knowledge in the culture of the soul. {6T 181.2}

"If you should allow the land near the school to be occupied with private houses and then be driven to select for cultivation other land at a distance from the school, it would be a great mistake and one always to be regretted. All the land near the building is to be regarded as the school farm, where the youth can be educated under well-qualified superintendents. The youth who shall attend our schools need all the land near by. They are to plant it with ornamental and fruit trees, and to cultivate garden produce. {6T 181.3}

"The school farm is to be regarded as a lessonbook in nature from which the teachers may draw their object lessons. Our students are to be taught that Christ, who created the world and all things that are therein, is the life and light of every living thing. The life of every child and youth who is willing to grasp the opportunities of receiving a proper education will be made thankful and happy while at school by the things upon which his eyes shall rest." {6T 181.4}

On several occasions the light has come to me that the land around our school is to be used as the Lord's farm. In a special sense portions of this farm should be highly cultivated. Spread out before me I saw land planted with every kind of fruit tree that will bear fruit in this locality; there were also vegetable gardens, where seeds were sown and cultivated. {6T 185.1}

If the managers of this farm and the teachers in the school will receive the Holy Spirit to work with them, they will have wisdom in their management, and God will bless their labors. The care of the trees, the planting and the sowing, and the gathering of the harvest are to be wonderful lessons for all the students. The invisible links which connect the sowing and the reaping are to be studied, and the goodness of God is to be pointed out and appreciated. It is the Lord that gives the virtue and the power to the soil and to the seed. Were it not for the divine agency, combined with human tact and ability, the seed sown would be useless. There is an unseen power constantly at work in man's behalf to feed and to clothe him. The parable of the seed as studied in the daily experience of teacher and student is to reveal that God is at work in nature, and it is to make plain the things of the kingdom of heaven. {6T 185.2}

The God of nature is perpetually at work. His infinite power works unseen, but manifestations appear in the effects which the work produces. The same God who guides the planets works in the fruit orchard and in the vegetable garden. He never made a thorn, a thistle, or a tare. These are Satan's work, the result of degeneration, introduced by him among the precious things; but it is through God's immediate agency that every bud bursts into blossom. When He was in the world in the form of humanity, Christ said: "My Father worketh hitherto, and I work." John 5:17. So when the students employ their time and strength in agricultural work, in heaven it is said of them, Ye "are laborers together with God." 1 Corinthians 3:9. {6T 186.2}

Let the lands near the school and the church be retained. Those who come to settle in Cooranbong can, if they choose, find for themselves homes near by, or on portions of, the Avondale estate. But the light given me is that all that section of land from the school orchard to the Maitland road, and extending on both sides of the road from the meetinghouse to the school, should become a farm and a park, beautiful with fragrant flowers and ornamental trees. There should be orchards, and every kind of produce should be cultivated that is adapted to the soil, that this place may become an object lesson to those living close by and afar off. {6T 187.1}

Then let everything not essential to the work of the school be kept at a distance, that the sacredness of the place may not be disturbed through the proximity of families and buildings. Let the school stand alone. It will be better for private families, however devoted they may be in the service of the Lord, to be located at some distance from the school buildings. The school is the Lord's property, and the grounds about it are His farm, where the Great Sower can make His garden a lessonbook. The results of the labors will be seen, "first the blade, then the ear, after that the full corn in the ear." Mark 4:28. The land will yield its treasures, bringing the joyousness of an abundant harvest; and the produce gathered through the blessing of God is to be used as nature's lessonbook, from which spiritual lessons can be made plain and applied to the necessities of the soul. {6T 187.2}

God's entrusted talents are not to be hid under a bushel or under a bed. "Ye are the light of the eath," Christ said. Matthew 5:14. As you see families living in hovels, with scant furniture and clothing, without tools, without books or other marks of refinement about their homes, will you become interested in them, and endeavor to teach them how to put their energies to the very best use, that there may be improvement, and that their work may move forward? It is by diligent labor, by putting to the wisest use every capability, by learning to waste no time, that they will become successful in improving their premises and cultivating their land. {6T 188.3}

Our schools must be conducted under the supervision of God. There is a work to be done for young men and women that is not yet accomplished. There are much larger numbers of young people who need to have the advantages of our training schools. They need the manual training course, that will teach them how to lead an active, energetic life. All kinds of labor must be connected with our schools.

Under wise, judicious, God-fearing directors the students are to be taught. Every branch of the work is to be conducted in the most thorough and systematic ways that long experience and wisdom can enable us to plan and execute. {6T 191.1}

"Let the teachers wake up to the importance of this subject, and teach agriculture and other industries that it is essential for the students to understand. Seek in every department of labor to reach the very best results. Let the science of the word of God be brought into the work, that the students may understand correct principles, and may reach the highest possible standard. Exert your God-given abilities, and bring all your energies into the development of the Lord's farm. Study and labor, that the best results and the greatest returns may come from the seed-sowing, that there may be an abundant supply of food, both temporal and spiritual, for the increased number of students that shall be gathered in to be trained as Christian workers." {6T 191.2}

February 5, 1901

It is God's desire that greater attention shall be paid to the spiritual necessities of the children and youth in the Healdsburg school, and in all our schools. When the managers of our schools make up their minds to carry out the principles which for years God has been presenting to them, they will be far better prepared to give attention to the spiritual needs of the students. {1MR 323.1}

If in the past, those in charge of the Healdsburg school had had spiritual foresight, they would have secured the land near the school home, which is now occupied by houses. The failure to furnish the students with outdoor employment, in the cultivation of the soil, is making their advancement in spirituality very slow and imperfect. The result of this neglect should lead the teachers to be wise unto salvation. It is a mistake for so many dwelling houses to be crowded close to the school home. This is working greatly to the disadvantage of the students. A lack of wisdom was shown by the failure to secure the land round the school home. This will make the work of preserving order and maintaining discipline harder than it otherwise would be. But order must be preserved at any cost, and the workers in the school must plan how this shall be done most successfully. Ms 11, 1901, pp. 6, 7. ("Words of Instruction to the Church at Healdsburg," February 5, 1901.) {1MR 323.2}

April 16, 1901

Satan gathered the fallen angels together to devise some way of doing the most possible evil to the human family. One proposition after another was made, till finally Satan himself thought of a plan. He would take the fruit of the vine, also wheat, and other things given by God as food, and would convert them into poisons, which would ruin man's physical, mental, and moral powers, and so overcome the senses that Satan should have full control. Under the influence of liquor, men would be led to commit crimes of all kinds. Through perverted appetite the world would be made corrupt. By leading men to drink alcohol, Satan would cause them to descend lower and lower in the scale. {RH, April 16, 1901 par. 7}

Satan has succeeded in turning the world from God. The blessings provided in God's love and mercy he has turned into a deadly curse. He has filled men with a craving for liquor and tobacco. This appetite, which has no foundation in nature, has destroyed its millions, yet it is indulged by high and low, rich and poor. Too often those appointed to guard the interests of the people are under the power of this appetite. {RH, April 16, 1901 par. 8}

June 29, 1901

It seems cruel to establish our schools in the cities, where the students are prevented from learning the precious lessons taught by nature. It is a mistake to call families into the city, where children and youth breathe an atmosphere of corruption and crime, sin and violence, intemperance and ungodliness. Oh, it is a terrible mistake to allow children to come in contact with that which makes such a fearful impression on their senses. Children and youth can not be too fully guarded from familiarity with the pictures of iniquity as common as in all large cities. {SpM 186.6}

Years ago schools should have been established on large tracts of land, where children could have been educated largely from the book of nature. Had this been done, what a different condition of things there would now be in our churches. We are in need of being uplifted, cleansed, purified. In our conversation we are altogether too cheap and common. There are tares growing among the wheat, and too often the tares overtop the wheat. {SpM 191.1}

I rejoiced when I heard that the Battle Creek School was to

be established in a farming district. I know that there will be less temptation there for the students than there would be in the cities that are fast becoming as Sodom and Gomorrah, preparing for destruction by fire. The popular sentiment is that cities should be chosen as locations for our schools. But God desires us to leave the sin-polluted atmosphere of the cities. It is his design that our schools shall be established where the atmosphere is purer. {SpM 191.2}

Note: Taken from Ms 67, 1901, p. 9. ("The Church School," typed July 29, 1901.) {6MR 408.1}

July 30, 1901

When Christ came to this world He found the Jewish people burdened with a heavy weight of traditions and ceremonies which the religious teachers had handed down from generation to generation. So great was the mass of tradition brought in that the commandments of God were made of none effect. Today there are those who are doing a work similar to that done by the Jewish teachers. They are dishonoring the law of God by their extreme teaching. There are those who say that nothing, not even insects, should be killed. God has not entrusted any such message to His people. It is possible to stretch the command "Thou shalt not kill" to any limit, but it is not according to sound reasoning to do this. Those who do it have not learned in the school of Christ. {20MR 338.1}

This earth has been cursed because of sin, and in these last days vermin of every kind will multiply. These pests must be killed, or they will annoy and torment and even kill us, and destroy the work of our hands and the fruit of our land. In places there are ants [termites] which entirely destroy the woodwork of houses. Should not these be destroyed? Fruit trees must be sprayed that the insects which would spoil the fruit may be killed. God has given us a part to act, and this part we must act with faithfulness. Then we can leave the rest with the Lord. {20MR 338.2}

God has given no man the message, Kill not ant or flea or moth. Troublesome and harmful insects and reptiles we must guard against and destroy, to preserve ourselves and our possessions from harm. And even if we do our best to exterminate these pests, they will still multiply. At camp meeting held at Brighton, Australia, the people were obliged to wear veils to keep the poisonous flies from their faces. While speaking, I was obliged to fan myself continually. {20MR 338.3}

As long as this life shall last, we shall have to fight the evils which have come in as a result of the curse. Evil will cease only when Satan ceases to exist. With the agencies which he has employed to annoy and grieve the people of God, Satan will at last be cast into the lake of fire and brimstone. Then sin will be no more. {20MR 338.4}

Those who advance the theory that vermin should not be killed know not of what they speak. There is nothing of this order in the teachings of Christ. It is not the Spirit of God that brings such theories as this to the mind. They originate with Satan who prepares every idle tale he can devise for the itching ears which cannot distinguish between truth and fiction. Discard all such theories for your own good and for the good of those with whom you associate. Those who go to such extremes do great harm. They bring the truth into disrepute. They place principles which are as precious as gold on a level with fables. Men might better let the fables rest in the silence of the grave than to speak and teach those things which have no foundation in the Word of God. {20MR 338.5}

August 13, 1901

Letters have come to me, asking in regard to the teaching of some who say that nothing that has life should be killed, not even insects, however annoying or distressing they may be. Is it possible that any one claims that God has given him this message to give to the people? The Lord has never given any human being such a message. God has told no one that it is a sin to kill the insects which destroy our peace and rest. In all His teaching, Christ gave no message of this character, and His disciples are to teach only what He commanded them. {RH, August 13, 1901 par. 1}

There are those who are always seeking to engage in controversy. This is the sum of their religion. They are filled with a desire to produce something new and strange. They dwell upon matters of the smallest consequence, exercising upon these their sharp, controversial talents. {RH, August 13, 1901 par. 2}

Idle tales are brought in as important truths, and by some they are actually set up as tests. Thus controversy is created, and minds are diverted from present truth. Satan knows that if he can get men and women absorbed in trifling details, greater questions will be left unheeded. He will furnish plenty of material for the attention of those who are willing to think upon trifling, unimportant subjects. The minds of the Pharisees were absorbed with questions of no moment. They passed by the precious truths of God's word to discuss the traditionary lore handed down from generation to generation, which in no way concerned their salvation. And so today, while precious moments are passing into eternity, the great questions of salvation are overlooked for some idle tale. {RH, August 13, 1901 par. 3}

I would say to my brethren and sisters, Keep close to the instruction found in the word of God. Dwell upon the rich truths of the Scriptures. Thus only can you become one in Christ. You have no time to engage in controversy regarding the killing of insects. Jesus has not placed this burden upon you. "What is the chaff to the wheat?" These side issues which arise are as hay, wood, and stubble compared with the truth for these last days. Those who leave the great truths of God's word to speak of such matters are not preaching the gospel. They are dealing with the idle sophistry which the enemy brings forward to divert minds from the truths that concern their eternal welfare. They have no word from Christ to vindicate their suppositions. {RH, August 13, 1901 par. 4}

December 27, 1901

There are times when things do not look as bright and cheerful as we could wish, because difficulties stand in the way of rapid advancement; but we hope, my brethren and sisters, that you will be encouraged to take a thorough interest in the establishment of the school at Berrien Springs, and aid it by the sale of "Christ's Object Lessons" and in other ways. Let the sale of "Christ's Object Lessons" be taken hold of interestedly in our large cities and in the smaller settlements. Brethren, wake up. The good hand of the Lord has been with our people in the selection of a good place to locate the school. This place corresponds to the representations given me as to where the school would be located. It is away from the cities, and there is an abundance of land for agricultural purposes, and room so that the houses will not need to be built one close to another. There is plenty of ground where students shall be educated to educate the land. "Ye are God's husbandry: ye are God's building." {SpM 203.5}

We would have all to understand when canvassing for "Object Lessons", that they are doing a work that is essential to be done for the school which should now be going on. The Lord will help each one who will pray and work, and work and pray. The light which I have tried to present before our people is that we must arouse ourselves from sleep, and feel an interest in the school that is to be built up at Berrien Springs. Do not let this matter of erecting suitable buildings fade away from your interest. It is for this purpose that the sale of "Object Lessons" should be vigorously carried forward. Let our prompt action enable the interested ones to make successful that work of moving our school out of Battle Creek. {SpM 204.1}

The land has been secured, and now the work of preparing suitable buildings is to be entered without delay. Let all plans be laid, and the fitting place be now selected. Let those who have been faithful workers take right hold and do their best. Let not this work fail. Let the students take right hold of this matter in earnest. Let not managers, teachers, or helpers swing back in their old customary ways of letting their influence negative the very plans the Lord has presented as the best plan for the physical, mental, and moral education of our youth. {SpM 204.2}

The Lord calls for steps in advance. Because the teachers may never have been trained to physical, manual labor, they are not easily persuaded in regard to the very best methods to secure for the youth an all-round education, and even the very ones who have been most reluctant to come into line in this matter, had they been given in their youth the physical, mental, and moral education combined, might have saved themselves several attacks of illness, and their brain, bone, and muscle would at this time be in a more healthy condition because all of the Lord's machine would be proportionately taxed. Precious lessons from the best instructors should be secured in spiritual lines, in agricultural employments, and also in carpenter's trade and in the printing business. The Lord would have these mechanical industries brought in and taught by competent men. {SpM 204.3}

Whoever shall take up the work of selling "Christ's Object Lessons" should have the help and encouragement of their brethren. {SpM 204.4}

1902

The great medical institutions in our cities, called sanitariums, do but a small part of the good they might do were they located where the patients could have the advantages of outdoor life. I have been instructed that sanitariums are to be established in many places in the country and that the work of these institutions will greatly advance the cause of health and righteousness. {7T 76.1}

The things of nature are God's blessings, provided to give health to body, mind, and soul. They are given to the well to keep them well and to the sick to make them well. Connected with water treatment, they are more effective in restoring health than all the drug medication in the world. {7T 76.2}

In the country the sick find many things to call their attention away from themselves and their sufferings. Everywhere they can look upon and enjoy the beautiful things of nature--the flowers, the fields, the fruit trees laden with their rich treasure, the forest trees casting their grateful shade, and the hills and valleys with their varied verdure and many forms of life. {7T 76.3}

And not only are they entertained by these surroundings, but at the same time they learn most precious spiritual lessons. Surrounded by the wonderful works of God, their minds are lifted from the things that are seen to the things that are unseen. The beauty of nature leads them to think of the matchless charms of the earth made new, where there will be nothing to mar the loveliness, nothing to taint or destroy, nothing to cause disease or death. {7T 76.4}

Nature is God's physician. The pure air, the glad sunshine, the beautiful flowers and trees, the orchards and vineyards, and outdoor exercise amid these surroundings, are health-giving--the elixir of life. Outdoor life is the only medicine that many invalids need. Its influence is powerful to heal sickness caused by fashionable life, a life that weakens and destroys the physical, mental, and spiritual powers. {7T 76.5}

How grateful to weary invalids accustomed to city life, the glare of many lights, and the noise of the streets are the quiet and freedom of the country! How eagerly do they turn to the scenes of nature!

How glad would they be for the advantages of a sanitarium in the country, where they could sit in the open air, rejoice in the sunshine, and breathe the fragrance of tree and flower! There are life-giving properties in the balsam of the pine, in the fragrance of the cedar and the fir. And there are other trees that are health-promoting. Let no such trees be ruthlessly cut down. Cherish them where they are abundant, and plant more where there are but few. {7T 77.1}

For the chronic invalid nothing so tends to restore health and happiness as living amid attractive country surroundings. Here the most helpless ones can be left sitting or lying in the sunshine or in the shade of the trees. They have only to lift their eyes and they see above them the beautiful foliage. They wonder that they have never before noticed how gracefully the boughs bend, forming a living canopy over them, giving them just the shade they need. A sweet sense of restfulness and refreshing comes over them as they listen to the murmuring breezes. The drooping spirits revive. The waning strength is recruited. Unconsciously the mind becomes peaceful, the fevered pulse more calm and regular. As the sick grow stronger, they will venture to take a few steps to gather some of the lovely flowers--precious messengers of God's love to His afflicted family here below. {7T 77.2}

Encourage the patients to be much in the open air. Devise plans to keep them out of doors, where, through nature, they can commune with God. Locate sanitariums on extensive tracts of land, where, in the cultivation of the soil, patients can have opportunity for healthful, outdoor exercise. Such exercise, combined with hygienic treatment, will work miracles in restoring and invigorating the diseased body and refreshing the worn and weary mind. Amid conditions so favorable the patients will not require so much care as if confined in a sanitarium in the city. Nor will they in the country be so much inclined to discontentment and repining. They will be ready to learn lessons in regard to the love of God, ready to acknowledge that He who cares so wonderfully for the birds and the flowers will care for the creatures formed in His own image. Thus opportunity is given physicians and helpers to reach souls, uplifting the God of nature before those who are seeking restoration to health. {7T 78.1}

In the night season I was given a view of a sanitarium in the country. The institution was not large, but it was complete. It was surrounded by beautiful trees and shrubbery, beyond which were orchards and groves. Connected with the place were gardens, in which the lady patients, when they chose, could cultivate flowers of every description, each patient selecting a special plot for which to care. Outdoor exercise in these gardens was prescribed as a part of the regular treatment. {7T 78.2}

Scene after scene passed before me. In one scene a number of suffering patients had just come to one of our country sanitariums. In another I saw the same company; but, oh, how transformed their appearance! Disease had gone, the skin was clear, the countenance joyful; body and mind seemed animated with new life. {7T 78.3}

I was also instructed that as those who have been sick are restored to health in our country sanitariums and return to their homes, they will be living object lessons, and many others will be favorably impressed by the transformation that has taken place in them. Many of the sick and suffering will turn from the cities to the country, refusing to conform to the habits, customs, and fashions of city life; they will seek to regain health in some one of our country sanitariums. Thus, though we are removed from the cities twenty or thirty miles, we shall be able to reach the people, and those who desire health will have opportunity to regain it under conditions most favorable. {7T 79.1}

God will work wonders for us if we will in faith co-operate with Him. Let us, then, pursue a sensible course, that our efforts may be blessed of heaven and crowned with success. {7T 79.2}

In August, 1901, while attending the Los Angeles camp meeting, I was in the visions of the night in a council meeting. The question under consideration was the establishment of a sanitarium in Southern California. By some it was urged that this sanitarium should be built in the city of Los Angeles, and the objections to establishing it out of the city were pointed out. Others spoke of the advantages of a country location. {7T 85.1}

There was among us One who presented this matter very clearly and with the utmost simplicity. He told us that it would be a mistake to establish a sanitarium within the city limits. A sanitarium should have the advantage of plenty of land, so that the invalids can work in the open air. For nervous, gloomy, feeble patients, outdoor work is invaluable. Let them have flower beds to care for. In the use of rake and hoe and spade they will find relief for many of their maladies. Idleness is the cause of many diseases. {7T 85.2}

Life in the open air is good for body and mind. It is God's medicine for the restoration of health. Pure air, good water, sunshine, the beautiful surroundings of nature--these are His means for restoring the sick to health in natural ways. To the sick it is worth more than silver or gold to lie in the sunshine or in the shade of the trees. {7T 85.3}

In the country our sanitariums can be surrounded by flowers and trees, orchards and vineyards. Here it is easy for physicians and nurses to draw from the things of nature lessons teaching of God. Let them point the patients to Him whose hand has made the lofty trees, the springing grass, and the beautiful flowers, encouraging them to see in every opening bud and blossoming flower an expression of His love for His children. {7T 85.4}

It is the expressed will of God that our sanitariums shall be established as far from the cities as is consistent. So far as possible these institutions should be located in quiet, secluded places, where opportunity will be afforded for giving the patients instruction concerning the love of God and the Eden home of our first parents, which, through the sacrifice of Christ, is to be restored to man. {7T 86.1}

In the effort made to restore the sick to health, use is to be made of the beautiful things of the Lord's creation. Seeing the flowers, plucking the ripe fruit, listening to the happy songs of the birds, has a peculiarly exhilarating effect on the nervous system. From outdoor life men, women, and children gain a desire to be pure and guileless. By the influence of the quickening, reviving, life-giving properties of nature's great medicinal resources the functions of the body are strengthened, the intellect awakened, the imagination quickened, the spirits enlivened, and the mind prepared to appreciate the beauty of God's word. {7T 86.2}

Under these influences, combined with the influence of careful treatment and wholesome food, the sick find health. The feeble step recovers its elasticity. The eye regains its brightness. The hopeless become hopeful. The once despondent countenance wears an expression of cheerfulness. The complaining tones of the voice give place to tones of content. The words express the belief: God is our refuge and strength, a very present help in trouble." Psalm 46:1. The clouded hope of the Christian is brightened. Faith returns. The word is heard: "Yea, though I walk through the valley of the shadow of death, I will fear no evil: for Thou art with me; Thy rod and Thy staff they comfort me." "My soul doth magnify the Lord, and my spirit hath rejoiced in God my Saviour." "He giveth power to the faint; and to them that have no might He increaseth strength." Psalm 23:4; Luke 1:46, 47; Isaiah 40:29. The acknowledgment of God's goodness in providing these blessings invigorates the mind. God is very near and is pleased to see His gifts appreciated. {7T 86.3}

February 5, 1902

In the night season I was taken from place to place, from city to city, in the Southern field. I saw the great work to be done--the work that ought to have been done years ago. We seemed to be looking at many places. Our first interest was for the places where the work has already been established, and for the places where the way has opened for a beginning to be made. I saw the places in the South where institutions have been established for the advancement of the Lord's work. One of the places that I saw was Graysville, and another [was] Huntsville. The Lord led in the establishment of these schools. Their work is not to be discouraged, but encouraged. They are to receive encouragement and support. Both of these places have advantages of their own. There has been delay in pushing forward the work in these places. Let us delay no longer. At these schools students may gain an education that, with the blessing of God, will prepare them to win souls to Christ. If they unite with the Saviour, they will grow in spirituality, and will be prepared to present the truth to others. {2MR 64.2}

We must provide greater facilities for the education and training of the youth, both white and colored. We are to establish schools away from the cities, where the youth can learn to cultivate the soil, and thus help to make themselves and the school self-supporting. Let means be gathered for the establishment of such schools. In connection with these schools, work is to be done in mechanical and agricultural lines. All the different lines of work that the situation of the place will warrant are to be brought in. {2MR 64.3}

Carpentering, blacksmithing, agriculture, the best way to make the most of what the earth produces--all these things are part of the education to be given to the youth.--Letter 25, 1902, pp. 8-9. (To Those in Positions of Responsibility in the Southern Field, Feb. 5, 1902.) {2MR 65.1}

February 26, 1902

The Lord will most surely impress minds in every place to devise means for the maintenance of the interests which are to feed the hungry, clothe the naked, and teach the ignorant, educating them in simple lines of book learning and in agriculture. He will give them wisdom to manufacture necessary, wholesome foods, which will be more needed in the Southern States than in any other part of America. He who feeds the ravens and cares for the wild beasts will give wisdom and skill, talent and ingenuity, for the production of wholesome foods, which are to be sold to the poor at as low a rate as possible. {HFM 57.3}

March 14, 1902

In the visions of the night I have been writing letters, and I dare not put off longer the work to be done. Night after night I am awakened at eleven, twelve, and one o'clock with a message from the Lord, and I arise at once and begin to write, fearing that if I do not, I shall forget the instruction given me. {17MR 348.1}

Thus it was when I was at Los Angeles. In the night season I was in a council meeting, and the question under consideration was the establishment of a sanitarium in Southern California. One brother urged that it would be best to have the sanitarium in the city of Los Angeles, and he pointed out the objections to establishing the sanitarium out of the city. {17MR 348.2}

There was among us One who presented this matter very clearly and with the utmost simplicity. He told us that it would be a mistake to establish a sanitarium within the city limits. A sanitarium should have the advantage of plenty of land, so that the invalids can work in the open air. For nervous, gloomy, feeble patients, out-of-door work is invaluable. Let them have flowerbeds to care for. In the use of rake and hoe and spade, they will find relief for many of their maladies. Idleness is the cause of many diseases. {17MR 348.3}

It need not be thought that there will be any disadvantage in establishing a sanitarium outside of the city. The establishment of a sanitarium ten, twenty, or even thirty miles from a city can not fail to be an advantage in every way, not a drawback. The patients can visit the city when they wish, but they are not obliged to remain in its smoke and dust and noise. {17MR 348.4}

When a sanitarium is established in the country, the sick can breathe the pure air of heaven. As they walk among the flowers and trees, joy and gladness fill their hearts. It is as if the smile of God were upon them, as they look upon the beautiful things He has created to bring joy to their sad hearts. {17MR 349.1}

Life in the open air is good for body and mind. It is God's medicine for the restoration of health. Pure air, good water, sunshine, beautiful surroundings--these are His means for restoring the sick to health in natural ways. {17MR 349.2}

The fact that in the country all these advantages can be obtained is a powerful incentive to the establishment of a sanitarium in the country. There the institution can be surrounded by flowers and trees, orchards and vineyard. The effect of such surroundings is, as it were, an elixir of life. {17MR 349.3}

It is worth more than silver or gold to sick people to lie in the sunshine or in the shade of the trees. And whenever opportunity offers, let those in charge of them draw lessons, teaching the love of God from the things of nature, from the lofty trees, the springing grass, and the beautiful flowers. Every opening bud and blossoming flower is an expression of God's love for His children. Point them upward to Him whose hand has made the beautiful things of nature. {17MR 349.4}

Christ points us to the things of nature, saying, "Consider the lilies of the field, how they grow; they toil not; neither do they spin; and yet I say unto you, That even Solomon in all his glory was not arrayed like one of these." From the trees, the running brooks, the stones, there are lessons to be learned. {17MR 349.5}

Whenever it is possible parents should have a piece of land connected with the home, that the children may learn to cultivate the soil. How many beautiful and valuable lessons may be drawn from preparing the ground, sowing the seed, and tending the growing plants. In learning these lessons, parents and children are benefited and blessed. {17MR 350.1}

The plagues of the last days are to be poured out on the inhabitants of the world who have shown marked contempt for the law of God. God's people should seek to reach the people of the world, proclaiming the truth as it is found in His Word. But the time will come when they will have to move away from the cities, and live in small companies, by themselves. {17MR 350.2}

If our people regard God's instruction as of value, they will move away from the city, so that they will not be pained by its revolting sights, and that their children will not be corrupted by its vices. Those who choose to remain in the cities, surrounded by the houses of unbelievers, must share the disaster that will come upon them. {17MR 350.3}

When the Lord was about to smite Egypt with hail, He said to Moses, "Behold, tomorrow about this time I will cause it to rain a very grievous hail, such as hath not been seen in Egypt since the foundation thereof until now. Send therefore now, and gather thy cattle, and all that thou hast in the field; for upon every man and beast that shall be found in the field, and shall not be brought home, the hail shall come down upon them, and they shall die" [Exodus 9:18, 19]. {17MR 350.4}

And before the destroying angel was sent to slay the firstborn of Egypt, Moses was told to say to the children of Israel, "Draw out and take you a lamb according to your families, and kill the passover. And ye shall take a bunch of hyssop, and dip it in the blood that is in the bason, and strike the lintel and the two sides posts with the blood that is in the bason; and none of you shall go out at the door of his house until morning. {17MR 350.5}

"For the Lord will pass through the land to smite the Egyptians; and when He seeth the blood upon the lintel, and on the two sideposts, the Lord will pass over the door, and will not suffer the destroyer to come in unto your houses to smite you" [verses 21-33]. The blood on the door was to be the sign that the Israelites were God's people. He who failed to obey would suffer with the Egyptians. The Lord could not spare him. {17MR 351.1}

Candid consideration is to be given to the matter of establishing a sanitarium in southern California. One thing is certain: This sanitarium is not to be established in the city. This I have said repeatedly. Establish it where there is ground for cultivation, where the patients can have opportunity for healthful exercise. Outdoor exercise, combined with hygienic treatment, will work miracles in restoring health to the sick. It is not according to the Lord's will to establish our sanitariums in the city. It may sometimes be necessary to begin the work in the city, but in such cases it should be carried on in rented buildings until a suitable location can be found outside the city. {17MR 351.2}

In Eden each day's labor brought to Adam and Eve health and gladness, and the happy pair greeted with joy the visits of their Creator, as in the cool of the day He walked and talked with them. Daily God taught them His lessons. {17MR 351.3}

The fruit of the tree of life in the garden of Eden possessed supernatural virtue. To eat of it was to live forever. Its fruit was the antidote for death. Its leaves were for the sustaining of life and immortality. But through man's disobedience death entered the world. Adam ate of the tree of the knowledge of good and evil, the fruit of which he had been forbidden to touch. This was his test. He failed, and his transgression opened the floodgates of woe upon the world. {17MR 351.4}

The tree of life was a type of the one great Source of immortality. Of Christ it is written, "In Him was life, and the life was the light of men." He is the fountain of life. Obedience to Him is the life-giving, vivifying power that gladdens the soul. Through sin man shut himself off from access to the tree of life. Now, life and immortality are brought to light through Jesus Christ. {17MR 352.1}

Christ declares, "I am the bread of life: he that cometh to Me shall never hunger; and he that believeth on Me shall never thirst." "Whoso eateth My flesh, and drinketh My blood, hath eternal life; and I will raise him up at the last day. For My flesh is meat indeed, and My blood is drink indeed....As the living Father hath sent Me, and I live by the Father; so he that eateth Me, even he shall live by Me. . . .The words that I speak unto you, they are spirit, and they are life." "To him that overcometh will I grant to eat of the tree of life, which is in the midst of the paradise of God." {17MR 352.2}

Why deprive the patients of the health-restoring blessing to be found in out-of-door life? I have been instructed that as the sick are encouraged to leave their rooms and spend time in the open air, tending the flowers or doing some other light, pleasant work, their minds will be called from self to something more health-giving. Open-air exercise should be prescribed as a beneficial, life-giving necessity. {17MR 352.3}

The longer patients can be kept out of doors, the less care they will require. The more cheerful their surroundings, the more hopeful they will be. Surround them with the beautiful things of nature, place them where they can see the flowers growing and hear the birds singing, and their hearts will break into song in harmony with the songs of the birds. Shut them in rooms and, be these rooms ever so elegantly furnished, they will grow fretful and gloomy. Give them the blessing of out-door life; for thus their souls will be uplifted, unconsciously and, in a large sense, consciously. Relief will come to body and mind. {17MR 352.4}

This return to God's original design is infinitely better than drug medication. All this was opened before me last night. I was awake from nine o'clock. Finding that I could not sleep, I dressed and asked the Lord to help me write out the instruction He had given me. {17MR 353.1}

I was referred to Ezekiel's vision of the mighty river. "These waters issued out toward the east country, and go down into the desert, and go into the sea; which being brought forth into the sea, the waters shall be healed. And it shall come to pass that every thing that liveth, which moveth, whithersoever the rivers shall come, shall live:. . . And the river upon the bank thereof, on this side and on that side, shall grow all trees for meat, whose leaf shall not fade, neither shall the fruit thereof be consumed; it shall bring forth new fruit according to his months, because their waters they issued out of the sanctuary; and the fruit thereof shall be for meat, and the leaf thereof for medicine" [Ezekiel 48:8, 9, 12]. Let all physicians be wise to learn. {17MR 353.2}

Grave mistakes have been made in establishing sanitariums in the city. I was instructed that our sanitariums should be established in the most pleasant surroundings, in places outside the city, where by wise instruction the thoughts of the patients can be bound up with the mind of God. Again and again I have described such places. But it seems that there has been no ear to hear. {17MR 353.3}

Last night in a most clear and convincing manner the mistakes now being made in our sanitarium work were presented to me. ....

Again and again I have been shown the advantage of establishing our institutions, especially sanitariums and schools, outside the city. To place our sanitariums where they are surrounded by ungodliness is to counterwork the efforts made to restore the patients to health. Many times in the past this has been presented to me. {17MR 354.1}

Our Redeemer is constantly working to restore in man the moral image of God. And although the whole creation groans under the curse, and fruit and flowers are nothing in comparison with what they will be in the earth made new, yet even today the sick may find health and gladness and joy in field and orchard. What a restorative this is! What a preventive of sickness! The leaves of the tree of life are for the healing of the believing, repenting children of God who avail themselves of the blessing to be found in tree and shrub and flower, even marred as nature is by the curse. {17MR 354.2}

July 6, 1902

The Lord will work upon human minds in unexpected quarters. Some who apparently are enemies of the truth will in God's providence invest their means to develop properties and erect buildings. In time, these properties will be offered for sale at a price far below their cost. Our people will recognize the hand of Providence in these offers, and will secure valuable properties for use in institutional work. They will plan and manage with humility, self-denial, and self-sacrifice. Thus men of means are unconsciously preparing auxiliaries that will enable the Lord's people to advance His work rapidly. {KC 72.3}

In various places properties are to be purchased to be used for sanitarium purposes. When opportunity offers, our people should purchase properties away from the cities, on which are buildings already erected and fruit orchards already in bearing. Land is a valuable possession. Connected with our sanitariums there should be lands, small portions of which can be used for the homes of the helpers and others who are receiving a training in medical missionary work. {KC 72.4}

Note: The same paragraphs appeared again a few months later in Testimonies for the Church vol. 7, p. 102.

July 10, 1902

During the General Conference, the way opened for the school to be moved from Battle Creek with the full approval of our people. {6MR 410.1}

Cautions were given to Brother Magan and Brother Sutherland against carrying their teaching so far above the spiritual line of education to which the students had been accustomed. They were told that the people were not prepared at once to understand and act intelligently upon the advanced light in regard to the Bible in education. I was instructed that they must advance steadily and solidly, and that they must guard against going to extremes in any line and against expressing their ideas in language that would confuse minds. Plain, simple language must be used. Instruction must be given line upon line, precept upon precept, here a little and there a little, leading the mind up slowly and intelligently. Every idea that they expressed must be clearly defined. {6MR 410.2}

They were told that unless they heeded this instruction, their teaching would result in a harvest of fanciful believers, who would not make straight paths for their feet, and who would look upon themselves as far ahead of all other Christians. In their teaching of truth, they were not to go so far in advance that it would be impossible for their students to follow them. Christ said to His disciples, "I have yet many things to say unto you, but ye cannot bear them now." {6MR 410.3}

I thank the Lord that the brethren heeded the instruction given them, and that they carried forward His work in simplicity and meekness, and yet intelligently. The Lord is qualifying them to teach the lessons He has given in His word, by object lessons from nature. This is the grandest, the most helpful, all-around education that the youth can have. Cultivating the soil, planting and caring for trees, sowing seed and watching its growth,--this work teaches precious lessons. Nature is an expositor of the word of the living God. But only through Christ does creation answer the highest purpose of the Creator. The Saviour has wonderful revelations for all who will walk humbly with God. Under the discipline and training of the higher teaching, they will behold wondrous things out of His law. {6MR 410.4}

In establishing schools, enough land should be secured to give the students opportunity to gain a knowledge of agriculture. If it is necessary to curtail the expense anywhere, let it be on the buildings. There should be no failure to secure land; for from the cultivation of the soil, the students are to learn lessons illustrating the truths of the word of God, truths that will help them to understand the work of the Creator. {6MR 411.1}

Those who have charge of the school at Berrien Springs have been learners in the school of Christ, and He has been working with them, preparing them to be acceptable teachers. It is right that they carry on the work they have begun. If they will watch unto prayer, and plead earnestly with God to supply them with His grace, they will increase in wisdom and knowledge. {6MR 411.2}

It has been a tremendous struggle for them to advance in the face of great financial embarrassment. They planned and contrived and devised in every way, with self-denial and self-sacrifice, to bring the school through, and to free it from its burden of debt. Now they begin to see that the way pointed out was the way of the Lord's leading. This is the lesson the Lord would have many more to learn. --Ms 98, 1902, pp. 5-10. ("Consideration to be Shown to Those Who in Their Work Have Wrestled with Difficulties," July 10, 1902.) {6MR 411.3}

September 17, 1902

A few days ago I had the privilege of seeing the buildings and the surroundings of the Fernando school. My time was very limited, but I was thankful for the opportunity of visiting the school-grounds. I am glad that you are several miles away from the city of Los Angeles. You have good buildings, and are in a favorable place for school work. I greatly desire that you shall make a right beginning. In planning for the erection of cottages for our brethren and sisters who may move there, be careful not to allow buildings to be put up too near the school property. Try to secure the land lying near the school, so that it will be impossible for houses to be built close to the campus. The land may be used for agricultural purposes. Later on, you may find it advisable to introduce various trades for the employment and training of the students; but at present about all that you can do is to teach them how to cultivate the land, so that it shall yield its fruit.-- Ms 54, 1903, pp. 1-4. ("The Work of Our Fernando School," Remarks, September 17, 1902.) {8MR 6.2}

November 13, 1902

In establishing schools, one important point is to secure land sufficient for the carrying forward of industries that will enable the students to be self-supporting. There should be land sufficient for the raising of the fruit and vegetables required by the school, and also some for sale. Agriculture should be made a financial benefit to the school. {PH151 76.3}

Nashville, Graysville, Huntsville, and Hildebran have been presented to me as places favorable for the raising of crops for the use of the school, and for marketing. {PH151 76.4}

The students in our schools are to be taught that which will prepare them to act their part in teaching others. Some are to learn one trade, some another. Some are specially adapted for the printing work. Such can be prepared to connect with the publishing work. {PH151 76.5}

The young men should learn to cultivate the soil, and to raise whatever the land will produce. No one can tell what can be done with the soil until he has studied, planned, and experimented. {PH151 76.6}

October 30, 1902

To parents who are living in the cities the Lord is sending the warning cry, Gather your children into your own houses; gather them away from those who are disregarding the commandments of God, who are teaching and practicing evil. Get out of the cities as fast as possible. {MM 310.3}

Parents can secure small homes in the country, with land for cultivation where they can have orchards and where they can raise vegetables and small fruits to take the place of flesh-meat, which is so corrupting to the lifeblood coursing through the veins. On such places the children will not be surrounded with the corrupting influences of city life. God will help His people to find such homes outside of the cities.--MS. 133, 1902. {MM 310.4}

November 17, 1902

Do not give the children playthings that are easily broken, and thus teach them lessons of destructiveness. The influence thus made upon their minds is not the most helpful to them. Let them have few playthings and let these be strong and durable. {10MR 325.5}

Such things, small though they may seem, mean much in the education of a child. When children reach a suitable age, they should be provided with tools. Both boys and girls should learn to use these tools. You will find them apt pupils. {10MR 325.6}

If the father is a carpenter, he should give his boys lessons in house-building, ever bringing into his instruction lessons from the Bible, the words of Scripture in which the Lord compares human beings to His building. {10MR 326.1}

If possible, let your home be out of the city, that your children may have ground to cultivate. Let them each have a piece of ground as their own, and as you teach them how to make a garden, how to prepare the soil for the seed, and the importance of keeping all the weeds pulled out, teach them how important it is to keep unsightly, injurious practices out of the life. Teach them to keep down wrong habits as they keep down the weeds in their gardens. It will take time to teach these lessons, but it will pay, yes, greatly pay. {10MR 326.2}

God demands of parents a faithful study of His Word and a determined effort to make a success of the church in the home. Then parents, with their converted children--the result of their obedience with God--can carry into the church their self-denial and sacrifice and their spiritual strength. {10MR 326.3}

The Lord created man out of the dust of the earth. He made Adam a partaker of His life, His nature. There was breathed into him the breath of the Almighty, and he became a living soul. Adam was perfect in form--strong, comely, pure, bearing the image of his Maker. God gave him a companion, a wife, to share with him the beauties of nature. In order for this holy pair to continue to be happy, God gave them something to do. The fact that they were holy did not debar them from working. God is never idle. To every one of the angelic host is given an appointed task. {10MR 326.4}

Adam and Eve were given the garden of Eden to care for. They were "to dress it and to keep it." They were happy in their work. Mind, heart, and will acted in perfect harmony. In their labor they found no weariness, no toil. Their hours were filled with useful work and communion with each other. Their occupation was pleasant. God and Christ visited them and talked with them. They were given perfect freedom. Only one restriction was placed on them. "Of every tree in the garden thou mayest freely eat," God said, "but of the tree of the knowledge of good and evil, thou shalt not eat of it; for in the day that thou eatest thereof thou shalt surely die" (Genesis 2:16, 17). {10MR 327.1}

This was the test of their obedience. God was the owner of their Eden home. They held it under Him.--Manuscript 102, 1903, pp. 8-12. ("Colaborers With Christ," November 17, 1902.)

1903

The education centering in the family was that which prevailed in the days of the patriarchs. For the schools thus established, God provided the conditions most favorable for the development of character. The people who were under His direction still pursued the plan of life that He had appointed in the beginning. Those who departed from God built for themselves cities, and, congregating in them, gloried in the splendor, the luxury, and the vice that make the cities of today the world's pride and its curse. But the men who held fast God's principles of life dwelt among the fields and hills. They were tillers of the soil and keepers of flocks and herds, and in this free, independent life, with its opportunities for labor and study and meditation, they learned of God and taught their children of His works and ways. {Ed 33.3}

In apportioning the inheritance of His people, it was God's purpose to teach them, and through them the people of after generations, correct principles concerning the ownership of the land. The land of Canaan was divided among the whole people, the Levites only, as ministers of the sanctuary, being excepted. Though one might for a season dispose of his possession, he could not barter away the inheritance of his children. When able to do so, he was at liberty at any time to redeem it; debts were remitted every seventh year, and in the fiftieth, or year of jubilee, all landed property reverted to the original owner. Thus every family was secured in its possession, and a safeguard was afforded against the extremes either of wealth or of poverty. {Ed 43.2}

By the distribution of the land among the people, God provided for them, as for the dwellers in Eden, the occupation most favorable to development--the care of plants and animals. A further provision for education was the suspension of agricultural labor every seventh year, the land lying fallow, and its spontaneous products being left to the poor. Thus was given opportunity for more extended study, for social intercourse and worship, and for the exercise of benevolence, so often crowded out by life's cares and labors. {Ed 43.3}

Were the principles of God's laws regarding the distribution of property carried out in the world today, how different would be the condition of the people! An observance of these principles would prevent the terrible evils that in all ages have resulted from the oppression of the poor by the rich and the hatred of the rich by the poor. While it might hinder the amassing of great wealth, it would tend to prevent the ignorance and degradation of tens of thousands whose ill-paid servitude is required for the building up of these colossal fortunes. It would aid in bringing a peaceful solution of problems that now threaten to fill the world with anarchy and bloodshed. {Ed 44.1}

By the casting of grain into the earth, the Saviour represents His sacrifice for us. "Except a corn of wheat fall into the ground and die." He says, "it abideth alone: but if it die, it bringeth forth much fruit." John 12:24. Only through the sacrifice of Christ, the Seed, could fruit be brought forth for the kingdom of God. In accordance with the law of the vegetable kingdom, life is the result of His death. {Ed 110.2}

So with all who bring forth fruit as workers together with Christ: self-love, self-interest, must perish; the life must be cast into the furrow of the world's need. But the law of self-sacrifice is the law of self-preservation. The husbandman preserves his grain by casting it away. So the life that will be preserved is the life that is freely given in service to God and man. {Ed 110.3}

The seed dies, to spring forth into new life. In this we are taught the lesson of the resurrection. Of the human body laid away to molder in the grave, God has said: "It is sown in corruption; it is raised in incorruption: it is sown in dishonor; it is raised in glory: it is sown in weakness; it is raised in power." 1 Corinthians 15:42, 43. {Ed 110.4}

As parents and teachers try to teach these lessons, the work should be made practical. Let the children themselves prepare the soil and sow the seed. As they work, the parent or teacher can explain the garden of the heart, with the good or bad seed sown there, and that as the garden must be prepared for the natural seed, so the heart must be prepared for the seed of truth. As the seed is cast into the ground, they can teach the lesson of Christ's death; and as the blade springs up, the truth of the resurrection. As the plant grows, the correspondence between the natural and the spiritual sowing may be continued. {Ed 111.1}

The youth should be instructed in a similar way. From the tilling of the soil, lessons may constantly be learned. No one settles upon a raw piece of land with the expectation that it will at once yield a harvest. Diligent, persevering labor must be put forth in the preparation of the soil, the sowing of the seed, and the culture of the crop. So it must be in the spiritual sowing. The garden of the heart must be cultivated. The soil must be broken up by repentance. The evil growths that choke the good grain must be uprooted. As soil once overgrown with thorns can be reclaimed only by diligent labor, so the evil tendencies of the heart can be overcome only by earnest effort in the name and strength of Christ. {Ed 111.2}

In the cultivation of the soil the thoughtful worker will find that treasures little dreamed of are opening up before him. No one can succeed in agriculture or gardening without attention to the laws involved. The special needs of every variety of plant must be studied. Different varieties require different soil and cultivation, and compliance with the laws governing each is the condition of success. The attention required in transplanting, that not even a root fiber shall be crowded or misplaced, the care of the young plants, the pruning and watering, the shielding from frost at night and sun by day, keeping out weeds, disease, and insect pests, the training and arranging, not only teach important lessons concerning the development of character, but the work itself is a means of development. In cultivating carefulness, patience, attention to detail, obedience to law, it imparts a most essential training. The constant contact with the mystery of life and the loveliness of nature, as well as the tenderness called forth in ministering to these beautiful objects of God's creation, tends to quicken the mind and refine and elevate the character. {Ed 111.3}

Children should not be long confined within doors, nor should they be required to apply themselves closely to study until a good foundation has been laid for physical development. For the first eight or ten years of a child's life the field or garden is the best schoolroom, the mother the best teacher, nature the best lesson book. Even when the child is old enough to attend school, his health should be regarded as of greater importance than a knowledge of books. He should be surrounded with the conditions most favorable to both physical and mental growth. {Ed 208.1}

With the question of recreation the surroundings of the home and the school have much to do. In the choice of a home or the location of a school these things should be considered. Those with whom mental and physical well-being is of greater moment than money or the claims and customs of society, should seek for their children the benefit of nature's teaching, and recreation amidst her surroundings. It would be a great aid in educational work could every school be so situated as to afford the pupils land for cultivation, and access to the fields and woods. {Ed 211.4}

In lines of recreation for the student the best results will be attained through the personal co-operation of the teacher. The true teacher can impart to his pupils few gifts so valuable as the gift of his own companionship. It is true of men and women, and how much more of youth and children, that only as we come in touch through sympathy can we understand them; and we need to understand in order most effectively to benefit. To strengthen the tie of sympathy between teacher and student there are few means that count so much as pleasant association together outside the schoolroom. In some schools the teacher is always with his pupils in their hours of recreation. He unites in their pursuits, accompanies them in their excursions, and seems to make himself one with them. Well would it be for our schools were this practice more generally followed. The sacrifice demanded of the teacher would be great, but he would reap a rich reward. {Ed 212.1}

No recreation helpful only to themselves will prove so great a blessing to the children and youth as that which makes them helpful to others. Naturally enthusiastic and impressible, the young are quick to respond to suggestion. In planning for the culture of plants, let the teacher seek to awaken an interest in beautifying the school grounds and the schoolroom. A double benefit will result. That which the pupils seek to beautify they will be unwilling to have marred or defaced. A refined taste, a love of order, and a habit of care-taking will be encouraged; and the spirit of fellowship and co-operation developed will prove to the pupils a lifelong blessing. {Ed 212.2}

So also a new interest may be given to the work of the garden or the excursion in field or wood, as the pupils are encouraged to remember those shut in from these pleasant places and to share with them the beautiful things of nature. {Ed 213.1}

Manual training is deserving of far more attention than it has received. Schools should be established that, in addition to the highest mental and moral culture, shall provide the best possible facilities for physical development and industrial training. Instruction should be given in agriculture, manufactures,--covering as many as possible of the most useful trades,--also in household economy, healthful cookery, sewing, hygienic dressmaking, the treatment of the sick, and kindred lines. Gardens, workshops, and treatment rooms should be provided, and the work in every line should be under the direction of skilled instructors. {Ed 218.1}

The work should have a definite aim and should be thorough. While every person needs some knowledge of different handicrafts, it is indispensable that he become proficient in at least one. Every youth, on leaving school, should have acquired a knowledge of some trade or occupation by which, if need be, he may earn a livelihood. {Ed 218.2}

The objection most often urged against industrial training in the schools is the large outlay involved. But the object to be gained is worthy of its cost. No other work committed to us is so important as the training of the youth, and every outlay demanded for its right accomplishment is means well spent. {Ed 218.3}

Even from the viewpoint of financial results, the outlay required for manual training would prove the truest economy. Multitudes of our boys would thus be kept from the street corner and the groggery; the expenditure for gardens, workshops, and baths would be more than met by the saving on hospitals and reformatories. And the youth themselves, trained to habits of industry, and skilled in lines of useful and productive labor--who can estimate their value to society and to the nation? {Ed 218.4}

As a relaxation from study, occupations pursued in the open air, and affording exercise for the whole body, are the most beneficial. No line of manual training is of more value than agriculture. A greater effort should be made to create and to encourage an interest in agricultural pursuits. Let the teacher call attention to what the Bible says about agriculture: that it was God's plan for man to till the earth; that the first man, the ruler of the whole world, was given a garden to cultivate; and that many of the world's greatest men, its real nobility, have been tillers of the soil. Show the opportunities in such a life. The wise man says, "The king himself is served by the field." Ecclesiastes 5:9. Of him who cultivates the soil the Bible declares, "His God doth instruct him to discretion, and doth teach him." Isaiah 28:26. And again, "Whoso keepeth the fig tree shall eat the fruit thereof." Proverbs 27:18. He who earns his livelihood by agriculture escapes many temptations and enjoys unnumbered privileges and blessings denied to those whose work lies in the great cities. And in these days of mammoth trusts and business competition, there are few who enjoy so real an independence and so great certainty of fair return for their labor as does the tiller of the soil. {Ed 219.1}

In the study of agriculture, let pupils be given not only theory, but practice. While they learn what science can teach in regard to the nature and preparation of the soil, the value of different crops, and the best methods of production, let them put their knowledge to use. Let teachers share the work with the students, and show what results can be achieved through skillful, intelligent effort. Thus may be awakened a genuine interest, an ambition to do the work in the best possible manner. Such an ambition, together with the invigorating effect of exercise, sunshine, and pure air, will create a love for agricultural labor that with many youth will determine their choice of an occupation. Thus might be set on foot influences that would go far in turning the tide of migration which now sets so strongly toward the great cities. {Ed 219.2}

Our schools could aid effectively in the disposition of the unemployed masses. Thousands of helpless and starving beings, whose numbers are daily swelling the ranks of the criminal classes, might achieve self-support in a happy, healthy, independent life if they could be directed in skillful, diligent labor in the tilling of the soil. {Ed 220.1}

For breaking the spell of fashion, the teacher can often find no means more effective than contact with nature. Let pupils taste the delights to be found by river or lake or sea; let them climb the hills, gaze on the sunset glory, explore the treasures of wood and field; let them learn the pleasure of cultivating plants and flowers; and the importance of an additional ribbon or ruffle will sink into insignificance. {Ed 247.6}

March 28, 1903

I look at these flowers, and every time I see them, I think of Eden. They are an expression of God's love for us. Thus He gives us in this world a little taste of Eden. He wants us to delight in the beautiful things of His creation, and to see in them an expression of what He will do for us. He wants us to live where we can have elbow room. His people are not to crowd into the cities. He wants them to take their families out of the cities, that they may better prepare for eternal life. In a little while they will have to leave the cities. These cities are filled with wickedness of every kind--with strikes and murders and suicides. Satan is in them, controlling men in their work of destruction. Under his influence they kill for the sake of killing, and this they will do more and more. Every mind is controlled either by the power of Satan or the power of God. If God controls our minds, what shall we be?--Christian gentlemen and Christian ladies. God can fill our lives with His peace and gladness and joy. He wants His joy to be in us, that our joy may be full. {12MR 30.3}

If we place ourselves under objectionable influences, can we expect God to work a miracle to undo the results of our wrong course? No, indeed. Get out of the cities as soon as possible, and purchase a little piece of land where you can have a garden, where your children can watch the flowers growing, and learn from them lessons of simplicity and purity. "Consider the lilies of the field, how they grow; they toil not, neither do they spin: And yet I say unto you, That even Solomon in all his glory was not arrayed like one of these" (Matthew 6:28, 29). Parents, point your children to the beautiful things of God's creation, and from these things teach them of His love for them. Point them to the lovely flowers--the roses and the lilies and the pinks--and then point them to the living God.--Ms. 10,

1903, pp. 11, 12. ("Lessons From Sending Out the Spies," March 28, 1903.) {12MR 31.1}

April 14, 1903

"Nashville is within easy access of Graysville and Huntsville, where a beginning of great value to the work in the South has been made. God has answered the many prayers offered in behalf of these two places. By the work in Nashville, the work in Graysville and Huntsville is to be confirmed, strengthened, and settled. Graysville and Huntsville are near enough to Nashville to strengthen the work there and to be strengthened by it. But it must be understood that we are to put forth special efforts to help the colored people. No longer is our indifference in this respect to continue. {GCB, April 14, 1903 par. 16}

"The schools in Graysville and Huntsville were established in the order of God. They are to do a work for Him. They are to become self-supporting, by making the best use of their land, by raising those products best suited to the climate and soil of their locality. Various industries are to be established. The Lord will greatly bless these industries if the workers will walk in His counsel. If they will look to Him, He will be their wisdom and their righteousness. His wisdom will be seen in the work of those who follow His directions. He will teach all who will learn of Him His meekness and lowliness." {GCB, April 14, 1903 par. 17}

The workers in the school at Huntsville are to have our tender sympathy and our practical aid. Do not let them suffer for the lack of facilities, for they are trying to educate the colored people. The school at Huntsville is in positive need of our care and our donations. {GCB, April 14, 1903 par. 18}

"The interests in Graysville and Huntsville will grow into usefulness, If the believers there will do their very best in the Lord's way. Let each one connected with the schools in these places remember that on him rests the responsibility of reflecting light to those in darkness. {GCB, April 14, 1903 par. 19}

Note: These four paragraphs appear in the midst of an article on the work in the Southern US. They comprise a smaller subsection and are quoted in full to maintain the context.

May 4, 1903

I have received instruction in regard to the college at Berrien Springs. The Lord said, If these, My servants, will walk humbly with contrite hearts, and will obey My voice, heeding the light I have given, I will grant them favor in the sight of men. I will not endorse the words of discouragement uttered by some of our leading men. {8MR 26.1}

The Lord instructed me that some connected with the institution would not see the necessity of uniting agricultural work with the instruction given in the school. In all our educational institutions physical and mental work should have been combined. In vigorous physical exercise, the animal passions find a healthy outlet and are kept in proper bounds. Healthful exercise in the open air will strengthen the muscles, encourage a proper circulation of blood, help to preserve the body from disease, and will be a great help in spirituality. For many years it has been presented to me that teachers and students should unite in this work. This was done anciently in the schools of the prophets.--Ms 40, 1903, p. 11. ("Perseverance in the Work of God," typed May 4, 1903.) Released May 20, 1977. {8MR 26.2}

July 5, 1903

My dear granddaughter, I feel a deep interest in you. I want you to have an experience that will be for your present and eternal good. Keep your heart stayed ever upon God. . . . {1MR 345.2}

The work of cultivating the heart is profitable at all times and in all places. "Ye are God's husbandry, ye are God's building" (1 Corinthians 3:9). We may learn a lesson from the work of the farmer in cultivating the field. He must cooperate with God. His part is to prepare the ground, and plant the seed, at the right time and in the right way. God gives the seed life. He sends the sunshine and the showers, and the seed springs up, "first the blade, then the ear, after that the full corn in the ear" (Mark 4:28). If the farmer fails to do his part, if the human agent does not cooperate with divine agencies, the sun may shine, the dew and the showers may fall upon the soil, but there will be no harvest. And though the work of planting had been done, unless God sent the sunshine and the dew and the rain, the seed would never, never spring up and grow. {1MR 345.3}

So, in the cultivation of character, you must cooperate with God.

His Word directs you to "work out your own salvation with fear and trembling. For it is God which worketh in you both to will and to do of His good pleasure" (Philippians 2:12, 13). You have a part to act, and as you act this part, God will surely cooperate with you. Letter 130, 1903, pp. 1,2. (To Miss Ella White, July 5, 1903.) {1MR 345.4}

August 9, 1903

My brethren and sisters, I ask you to give the school at Healdsburg your sympathy and support. Do not become weary in well-doing. In carrying forward the work of selling "Christ's Object Lessons," you will receive a most precious blessing. {PH164 37.1}

I urge that our other schools be given encouragement in their efforts to develop plans for the training of the youth in agricultural and other lines of industrial work. When, in ordinary business, pioneer work is done, and preparation is made for future development, there is frequently a financial loss. And as our schools introduce manual training, they, too, may at first incur loss. But let us remember the blessing that physical exercise brings to the students. Many students have died while endeavoring to acquire an education, because they confined themselves too closely to mental effort. {PH164 37.2}

We must not be narrow in our plans. In industrial training there are unseen advantages, which can not be measured or estimated. Let no one begrudge the effort necessary to carry forward successfully the plan that for years has been urged upon us as of primary importance. {PH164 37.3}

August 26, 1903

Had the sanitarium been re-established in accordance with the Lord's design, it would not now be in Battle Creek. The Lord permitted the sanitarium to be destroyed by fire, to take away the objection raised to moving out of Battle Creek. It was His design, not that one large building should be erected, but that plants should be made in several places. These smaller sanitariums were to be established where they could have the benefit and advantage of land for agricultural purposes. It is God's plan that agriculture shall be carried on in connection with our sanitariums and schools. Our youth need the education to be gained from this line of work. It is well, and more than well--it is essential--that efforts be made to carry out the Lord's plan in this respect. {11MR 42.2}

When the call came to move out of Battle Creek, the plea was made, "We are here, and all settled. It would be an impossibility to move without enormous expense." {11MR 43.1}

The Lord permitted fire to consume the sanitarium building, and thus removed the greatest objection to fulfilling His purpose. Then a large building, different in design, but capable of accommodating as many patients, was erected on the same site as the old building. Since the opening of this institution a very large number of people have come to it. Some of these are patients, but some are merely tourists. But the large number at the sanitarium is no evidence that it is the will of God that such a condition of things should be. Our sanitariums were not designed to be boarding places for rich people of the world. {11MR 43.2}

Note: Extracted from a letter written to Frederick Griggs regarding the work in Battle Creek. The Battle Creek Sanitarium was burned to the ground on Feb. 18, 1902. The Review and Herald would be destroyed by fire later that year on Dec. 30.

September, 1903

I have received much instruction regarding the location of sanitariums. They should be a few miles distant from the large cities, and land should be secured in connection with them. Fruit and vegetables should be cultivated, and the patients should be encouraged to take up outdoor work. Many who are suffering from pulmonary disease might be cured if they would live in a climate where they could be out-of-doors most of the year. Many who have died of consumption might have lived if they had breathed more pure air. Fresh outdoor air is as healing as medicine, and leaves no injurious aftereffects.... {2SM 291.1}

It would have been better if, from the first, all drugs had been kept out of our sanitariums, and use had been made of such simple remedies as are found in pure water, pure air, sunlight, and some of the simple herbs growing in the field. These would be just as efficacious as the drugs used under mysterious names, and concocted by human science. And they would leave no injurious effects in the system. {2SM 291.2}

Thousands who are afflicted might recover their health if, instead of depending upon the drugstore for their life, they would discard all drugs, and live simply, without using tea, coffee, liquor, or spices, which irritate the stomach and leave it weak, unable to digest even simple food without stimulation. The Lord is willing to let His light shine forth in clear, distinct rays to all who are weak and feeble.-- Manuscript 115, 1903 (General Manuscript regarding sanitarium work). {2SM 291.3}

Note: Manuscript 112 was written on Aug. 22, 1903 and Ms. 117 was written on Sept. 24, 1903.

September, 1903

As I consider the state of things in Battle Creek, I tremble for our youth who go there. The light given me by the Lord, that our youth should not collect in Battle Creek to receive their education, has in no particular changed. The fact that the sanitarium has been rebuilt does not change the light. That which in the past has made Battle Creek a place unsuitable for the education of our youth makes it unsuitable today so far as influence is concerned. {8T 227.1}

When the call came to move out of Battle Creek, the plea was: "We are here, and all settled. It would be an impossibility to move without enormous expense." {8T 227.2}

The Lord permitted fire to consume the principal buildings of the Review and Herald and the sanitarium, and thus removed the greatest objection urged against moving out of Battle Creek. It was His design that instead of rebuilding the one large sanitarium, our people should make plants in several places. These smaller sanitariums should have been established where land could be secured for agricultural purposes. It is God's plan that agriculture shall be connected with the work of our sanitariums and schools. Our youth need the education to be gained from this line of work. It is well, and more than well,--it is essential,--that efforts be made to carry out the Lord's plan in this respect. {8T 227.3}

1904 – Nashville Agricultural and Normal Institute (Madison) Opened, Washington Missionary College Opened

January 8, 1904

(Written January 8, 1904, from "Elmshaven," Sanitarium, California, "To the Brethren and Sisters Connected With the Medical Work in Southern California.")

I have read the letters that have been written to me regarding sanitarium sites in southern California, and I will now try to write some things that have been presented to me for you. {19MR 229.1}

The furnished building in Pomona, offered for twenty-five thousand dollars, is in some respects favorable for sanitarium work. In other respects it does not answer to the representation given me of what our sanitariums should be. More land would be needed. The time is fast coming when the controlling power of the labor unions will be very oppressive. {19MR 229.2}

Again and again the Lord has instructed that our people are to take their families away from the cities, into the country, where they can raise their own provisions; for in the future the problem of buying and selling will be a very serious one. We should now begin to heed the instruction given us over and over again: Get out of the cities into rural districts, where the houses are not crowded closely together, and where you will be free from the interference of enemies. {19MR 229.3}

Our sanitariums should not be situated in or near any city. And it is most important that in connection with them land be secured, that homes may be provided for those who help in the institution, and also that facilities for outdoor work be provided for the patients. {19MR 229.4}

Let houses be built for families who have not a firm hold of life. Let men and women work in fields and orchard and garden. This will bring health and strength to nerve and muscle. Living indoors and cherishing invalidism is a very poor business. If those who are sick will give nerves and muscles and sinews proper exercise in the open air, their health will be renewed. {19MR 230.1}

The most astonishing ignorance prevails in regard to putting brain, bone, and muscle into active service. Every part of the human organism should be equally taxed. This is necessary for the harmonious development and action of every part. {19MR 230.2}

Many do not see the importance of having land to cultivate, and of raising fruit and vegetables, that their tables may be supplied with these things. I am instructed to say to every family and every church, God will bless you when you work out your own salvation with fear and trembling, fearing lest, by unwise treatment of the body, you will mar the Lord's plan for you. {19MR 230.3}

Many act as if health and disease were things entirely independent of their conduct, and entirely outside their control. They do not reason from cause to effect, and submit to feebleness and disease as a necessity. Violent attacks of sickness they believe to be special dispensations of Providence, or the result of some overruling, mastering power; and they resort to drugs as a cure for the evil. But the drugs taken to cure the disease weaken the system. If those who are sick would exercise their muscles daily, women as well as men, in outdoor work, using brain, bone, and muscle proportionately, weakness and languor would disappear. Health would take the place of disease, and strength the place of feebleness. {19MR 230.4}

Let those who are sick do all in their power, by correct practice in eating, drinking, and dressing, and by taking judicious exercise, to secure recovery of health. Let the patients who come to our sanitariums be taught to cooperate with God in seeking health. "Ye are God's husbandry, ye are God's building." God made nerve and muscle in order that they might be used. It is the inaction of the human machinery that brings suffering and disease. {19MR 231.1}

A few words more in regard to the location of our sanitariums. Never, never should these institutions be established in the cities. They should be established in the country, amidst pleasant surroundings and in connection with plenty of land. This is a positive necessity. Flower- and vegetable-gardens and orchards will be found to be health-giving agencies in the successful treatment of the sick. Many who come to our sanitariums to receive the benefit of these advantages will be blessed with improved health. So interested will they become in the work given them to do that they will forget their aches and pains. {19MR 231.2}

It is because there is so little land in connection with this property at Pomona, that I seriously question the advisability of purchasing it. Land we must have, that the patients may be provided with outdoor employment. {19MR 231.3}

The Potts' Sanitarium, which is situated five miles out of San

Diego, is now offered to us at a very low price. If I were younger, I should be strongly inclined to take that property, and try to build up sanitarium work there. If we do not improve such opportunities, we may never find anything better. There are always some risks to run. This has been our experience from the beginning of the work until now. {19MR 231.4}

My son has just let me read the letters that he has written to you, and what he says meets my mind. I will not write any more now, but if further light comes to me, will send it to you.--Letter 5, 1904. {19MR 231.5}

April 26, 1904

There is a special work to be done at this time,--a work of great importance. Light has been given me that a sanitarium should be established near Los Angeles, in some rural district. For years the need of such an institution has been kept before our people in Southern California. Had the brethren there heeded the warnings given by the Lord, to guard them from making mistakes, they would not now be tied up as they are. But they have not followed the instruction given. They have not gone forward in faith to establish a sanitarium near Los Angeles. {1MR 255.3}

The buildings secured for this work should be out of the cities, in the country, so that the sick may have the benefit of outdoor life. By the beauty of flower and field, their minds will be diverted from themselves, from their aches and pains, and they will be led to look from nature to the God of nature, who has provided so abundantly the beauties of the natural world. The convalescent can lie in the shade of the trees, and those who are stronger can, if they wish, work among the flowers, doing just a little at first, and increasing their efforts as they grow stronger. Working in the garden, gathering flowers and fruit, listening to the birds praising God, the patients will be wonderfully blessed. Angels of God will draw near to them. They will forget their sorrows. Melancholy and depression will leave them. The fresh air and sunshine, and the exercise taken, will bring them life and vitality. The wearied brain and nerves will find relief. Good treatment and a wholesome diet will build them up and strengthen them. They will feel no need for health-destroying drugs or for intoxicating drink. {1MR 255.4}

It is the purpose of God that a sanitarium shall be established at some suitable place near Los Angeles. This institution is to be managed carefully and faithfully, by men who have clear spiritual discernment and who have, also, financial ability.--men who can carry the work forward successfully, as faithful stewards. {1MR 256.1}

We are to labor under the counsel of the great Master Workman. In His strength human beings can and will follow a course of action that will win souls to Christ. Letter 147, 1904, pp. 1-5. (To Brother Bowles, April 26, 1904.) {1MR 256.2}

May 10, 1904

I have just read your letter to Willie. Thank you for writing. You will not be surprised when I tell you that I miss you all very much. Separation does not mean forgetting. {16MR 185.2}

I am glad to hear that you have bought a horse, and that you are pleased with him. I hope that he will work as well in the buggy as he does on the farm. {16MR 185.3}

Could you not try the Hizerman boy on the farm? I am anxious that he shall be helped. But do as your judgment says in regard to this. {16MR 185.4}

It seems very much like home here, with open ground all around us, and the cherry trees in full bloom behind the house. But we cannot look forward to having sweet corn and tomatoes from the place as we could were we at home. But we will not wish ourselves at home. We must feel grateful for this pleasant place. Still, it is well that no others came with us. They would miss the conveniences and comforts of home. {16MR 185.5}

The work on our buildings [ACCORDING TO THE REVIEW AND HERALD, APRIL 28, 1904, THE "BUILDINGS" INCLUDED "THE SANITARIUM, TRAINING-SCHOOL, AND GENERAL CONFERENCE OFFICES IN WASHINGTON, D. C."] will soon begin in earnest. It has taken till the end of last week to get all the business arrangements completed, leaving nothing at loose ends. We hope that now steady advancement will be made. Four good horses have been purchased to do the teaming and the necessary work on the land to prepare it for the buildings. {16MR 185.6}

I pray that the Lord will help in every line of work, in every business transaction, that the principles of Christ may be carried out. There must be no unfair dealing. God's workers are to do to others as they would be done by. It has been most painful to see those who profess to believe present truth following in their business transactions a course directly opposed to the directions that the Lord gave Moses to give to the children of Israel. We are to carry out these principles. We are to be representatives of truth and righteousness. We are called to be sons and daughters of God, to live the Christ-life. {16MR 186.1}

May the Lord bless you abundantly, my brother, in your home. The charge I have to give you is: Do not load yourself down with so many burdens that you will fail to do your duty to your children. I do not write these words as a reproach, but as a reminder. If anything must be neglected, let it be the care of inanimate things. Keep your own soul fresh and pure and uplifted. If you give your children the attention they need, some things may have to be neglected. Then let them be. Your children are building characters for time and for eternity, and you must make no mistakes in dealing with them. Be assured that I will not censure you for anything left undone on the farm. {16MR 186.2}

May the peace of God abide in your home. May His blessing rest upon your little flock. They are lambs of His fold, and must be nurtured and cherished. Do not overwork. Do not strain every nerve and muscle to try to do everything that there is to do on the farm, but get help. {16MR 186.3}

May the Lord abundantly bless you and your wife and children.--Letter 159, 1904. {16MR 187.1}

Note: Personal letter written to Iram James.

June 10, 1904

The farm should have careful husbandry. We are sorry that Brother Jacobs has been obliged to leave Huntsville. He has left, not because of unfaithfulness or inefficiency, but because of the condition of his health and the feebleness of Sister Jacobs, brought on by hard work. Brother and Sister Jacobs should have had the help of others who were spiritual minded and intelligent. It may be that if proper facilities are provided to make the labor on the farm less taxing, Brother Jacobs might be encouraged to return and resume his work. If he should return, however, he should have able assistants to work with him. {PCO 118.2}

The Huntsville School has been presented to me as being in a very desirable location. It would be difficult to secure another location as promising as the school farm now secured. The buildings and everything connected with the work there should be in harmony with the high and sacred work to be done there. Let there be nothing unsightly connected with the buildings or about the farm, nothing that would indicate slackness. {PCO 118.5}

If the land is well cared for, it will produce abundantly. Let the teachers go out, taking with them small companies of students, and teach these students how properly to work the soil. Let all those connected with the school study to see how they may improve the property. Teach the students to keep the gardens free from weeds. Let each one see that his room is clean and presentable. Let the care and cultivation of the land of the Huntsville School show to unbelievers that Seventh-day Adventists are reliable and that their influence is of value in the community. The sight of a farm, unproductive because of neglect, has a tendency to belittle the influence of the school. {PCO 119.1}

The farm, if worked intelligently, is capable of furnishing fruit and other produce for the school. The teachers, both in their work in the schoolroom and on the farm, should constantly seek to reach a higher standard, that they may be better able to teach the students how to care for the trees, the berries, the vegetables, and the grains that shall be raised. This will be pleasing to God and will bring the approval and respect of those in the community who understand the principles of agriculture. {PCO 119.2}

So much work of a faulty nature has been done in the school at Huntsville that it will now require stern efforts to restore the work to healthfulness, but such efforts should be put forth. Many discouragements have come in, but the Lord will let His blessing rest upon those who will take hold of the work thoroughly and in earnest. There is a special need of intense earnestness. Take hold with heart and mind and strength to redeem the farm, that it may be, as it has been presented to me, a beautiful place, well pleasing to the

Lord, a spectacle to angels and to men. {PCO 119.5}

We hope that the present sickly appearance may give place to healthful conditions. Careful cultivation will bring good returns, and the sad lack now seen may be overcome by the exercise of intelligence in determining what must be done. Let us remember that the land is God's property to be worked energetically to His glory. The trees and grains and vegetables will yield their fruit in proportion to the labor that is put forth in their care. {PCO 119.6}

The talents entrusted to the keeping of those in the school have not been diligently put out to the exchangers. The character of much of the work has left an unfavorable impression upon the minds of unbelievers. It is time now to take up the work in faith and prayer with all the capabilities God has given. Cultivate the land and it will produce its treasures. Turn to God in faith, working as under the eye of the great Searcher of hearts. Let each worker encourage the one next to him, each holding up the hands of each, all yielding obedience to God's requirements. {PCO 120.3}

As believers in the greatest truths ever given to mortals, we should put to the highest use the talents that God has entrusted to us. The farm and the school at Huntsville have been placed in our hands as a precious treasure. We cannot express in words all that is involved in the proper cultivation of the land and the education of the students in domestic duties. If this work is done in the fear of God, souls will be influenced to take their position on the side of an unpopular truth. {PCO 120.4}

Let none of our schools be conducted in a cheap, careless manner. He that is faithful in that which is least will be faithful also in that which is greater. If little things are left uncorrected, there is danger that larger evils will be regarded indifferently. The faithful steward of the Lord's treasure will correct at once the small mistakes. Whether his duties are connected with the cultivation of the Lord's land, or with the buildings that are erected on the land, he will do every stroke well. The Lord will take notice of his faithfulness, and He will strengthen the ability to plan and execute in temporal matters. And this faithful exactitude is a special necessity where eternal interests are involved. {PCO 121.1}

Many persons have not been educated to care for the little things. Yet such an education is necessary to success. Those who reach a high standard must overcome the tendency to slothfulness. A tendency to neglect something that should be done at once grows into a habit of indolence. See that broken plastering, broken furniture, or broken carriages are promptly put in repair. Slothfulness in character is demoralizing. {PCO 121.5}

The horses should have the best of care. The vehicles and the harness must be kept in good repair that lives be not imperiled. Keep the harness well oiled. {PCO 121.6}

Several acres of land should at the right time be set out to tomatoes. Young plants should be ready to be transplanted as early as possible. Such a crop would be valuable and might be used to good advantage. Let everything reveal religious thrift. {PCO 121.7}

There will be disagreeable tasks to be performed. Let no duty be overlooked, with the expectation that someone else will perform it. Let there be no superficial work done in any part of the school. Take hold of the forbidding task, and master it, and thus you will obtain a victory. The putting off even of little duties weakens the habits of promptness that should be encouraged. Cultivate the habit of seeing what ought to be done, and do it promptly. If a board is broken in the walk, do not leave it for someone else to repair. Let each one feel a responsibility for the care of the premises. Overcome natural indolence. Do not neglect the disagreeable things, supposing that they will be attended to by someone else. All these rules are important for the formation of right character. {PCO 122.1}

June 17, 1904

What we need to keep the bodily machinery in running order is the physical and mental taxation combined so that all parts will be taxed proportionately. You go and sit down and study, study, study. I have known it to lay many in the grave. {SpM 355.4}

Every portion of the living machinery is to act its part. That is why in Berrien Springs they came out here to clear the land, that the youth may have a fair understanding of what true education is, and we want all to help this work. {SpM 355.5}

Now, I am very thankful that a work has been done here in Berrien Springs, and it might be done a hundred places where there is one if there will be those who have the moral courage to take the Word of God and to practice it. {SpM 357.3}

The Lord was in this school's being established. The Lord helped these brethren as they progressed with their school, and as they were teaching the very principles that were taught in the schools of the prophets. Do you think in the schools of the prophets they went back to all those books that are brought into the school to give an education? Do you think they took the study books that were in the common schools? No, No! What were they taught? To have a knowledge of Jesus Christ. If they have a practical knowledge of Jesus Christ, let me tell you, they understand that they must be partakers of the divine nature in order to escape corruption that is in the world through lust, and come out of the cities. It is the very thing to do today. Get them out of the cities into the rural places, where they may be educated in agriculture and the various lines of business and trade. Do you suppose that when the times are growing worse and worse that you will all be left together here in one company? No, we shall be scattered. If those who are helping educate in this place shall give the right kind of education, these students will be qualified to go out into new places and begin with ABC work to educate others. As they commence, the Holy Spirit of God will stand by their side. {SpM 357.4}

June 20, 1904

The plan upon which our brethren propose to work is to select some of the best and most substantial young men and women from Berrien Springs and other places in the North, who believe that God has called them to the work in the South, and give them a brief training as teachers. Thorough instruction will be given in Bible study, physiology, and the history of our message; and special instruction in agriculture will be given. It is hoped that many of these students will eventually connect with schools in various places in the South. In connection with these schools there will be land that will be cultivated by teachers and students, and the proceeds from this work will be used for the support of the schools. {RH, August 18, 1904 par. 14}

We went once more to see the farm, after its purchase had been completed, and were very much pleased with it. I earnestly hope that the school to be established there will be a success, and will help to build up the work of the Lord in that part of his vineyard. There are men of means in various parts of the land who can assist this enterprise by loans without interest, and by liberal gifts. {RH, August 18, 1904 par. 15}

Note: These paragraphs appear in 11MR p. 166 where it is stated that they were originally written to Miss M.A. Davis on June 20, 1904.

June 21, 1904

In regard to this school here at Huntsville, I wish to say that for the past two or three years I have been receiving instruction in regard to it-- what it should be, and what those who come here as students are to become. All that is done by those connected with this school, whether they be white or black, is to be done with the realization that this is the Lord's institution, in which the students are to be taught how to cultivate the land, and how to labor for the uplifting of their own people. They are to work with such earnestness and perseverance that the farm will bear testimony, to the world, to angels, and to men, to the fidelity with which this donation of land has been cared for. This is the Lord's land, and it is to bear fruit to His glory. Those who attend this school, to be taught in right lines, on the farm or in the school, are to live in close connection with God. {6MR 211.1}

I feel so grateful that we have this farm on which to carry on our school work. I am so glad that it is land which will produce. But it cannot be expected to produce fruit if it is left uncultivated. From this we may learn a spiritual lesson. "It is My Father's good pleasure," Christ says to His disciples, "that ye bear much fruit." But you cannot bear much fruit unless you take out of your lives the weeds of evil, and let the word of truth dwell in you richly, that your lives may produce the fruits of righteousness and holiness. If you will do this, you will see in the kingdom of God the result of what you have learned on this school farm. Pull up the weeds, and plant the seeds of truth. . . . {6MR 213.2}

I say again, I am so glad that we have this farm. One came to me, and said, "I think it is a mistake to keep that land. It is not half cultivated. I think that they might better turn it back to the Conference." That night instruction was given me regarding the matter. It was God's purpose that the school should be placed here. He saw that the workers here would not have to fight every inch of the ground, as the workers in some places have had to do, in order to establish the truth. The instruction was given me, Never, never part with an acre of this land. It is to educate hundreds. If those who come here as teachers will do their part, if they will take up their work in God's name, sending their petitions to heaven for light and grace and strength, success will attend their efforts. The teachers are to be kind and tender, and at the same time very thorough in discipline. This is most essential. {6MR 214.3}

Note: These paragraphs are part of a talk given at Oakwood College on June 21, 1904.

June 30, 1904

Early on Monday morning [June 20, 1904] we took the train for Huntsville. We reached the school at one o'clock the same day. That afternoon we were taken over a portion of the school farm. We find that there are nearly four hundred acres of land, a large part of which is under cultivation. Several years ago Brother S. M. Jacobs was in charge of the farm, and under his care it made great improvement. He set out a peach and plum orchard, and other fruit trees. Brother and Sister Jacobs left Huntsville about three years ago, and since then the farm has not been so well cared for. We see in the land promise of a much larger return than it now gives, were its managers given the help they need. {2MR 67.1}

Brother Jacobs put forth most earnest, disinterested efforts, but he was not given the help that his strength demanded. Sister Jacobs also worked very hard, and when her health began to give way, they decided to leave Huntsville and go to some place where the strain would not be so heavy. Had they then been furnished with efficient helpers and with the means necessary to make the needed improvements, the advancement made would have given Brother Jacobs encouragement. But the means that ought to have gone to

Huntsville did not go, and we see the result in the present showing. {2MR 67.2}

Recently the suggestion has been made that the school at Huntsville is too large, and perhaps it would be better to sell the property there and establish the school elsewhere. But in the night season instruction was given me that this farm must not be sold. The Lord's money was invested in the Huntsville school farm to provide a place for the education of colored students. The General Conference gave this land to the Southern work, and the Lord has shown me what this school may become and what those may become who go there for instruction, if His plans are followed. {2MR 67.3}

There is need at the Huntsville school of a change in the faculty. There is need of money, and of sound, intelligent generalship, that things may be well kept up, and that the school may give evidence that Seventh-day Adventists mean to make a success of whatever they undertake. {2MR 68.1}

Wise plans are to be laid for the cultivation of the land. The students are to be given a practical education in agriculture. This education will be of inestimable value to them in their future work. Thorough work is to be done in cultivating the land, and from this the students are to learn how necessary it is to do thorough work in cultivating the garden of the heart. {2MR 68.2}

The facilities necessary for the success of the school must be provided. At present the facilities are very meager. There is not a bathroom on the premises. A small building should be put up, in which the students can be taught how to care for one another in time of sickness. There has been a nurse at the school to look after the students when they were sick, but no facilities have been provided. This has made the work very discouraging. {2MR 68.3}

The students are to be given a training in those lines of work that will help them to be successful laborers for Christ. They are to be taught to be separate from the customs and practices of the world. They are to be taught how to present the truth for this time, and how to work with their hands and with their heads to win their daily bread, that they may go forth to teach their own people. The bread-winning part of the work is of the utmost importance. They are to be taught also to appreciate the school as a place in which they are given opportunity to obtain a training for service. {2MR 68.4}

The teachers should constantly seek wisdom from on high, that they may be kept from making mistakes. They should give careful consideration to their work, that each student may be prepared for the line of service to which he is best adapted. All are to be prepared to serve faithfully in some capacity. {2MR 69.1}

No laxness is to be allowed. The man who takes charge of the Huntsville School should know how to govern himself and how to govern others. The Bible teacher should be a man who can teach the students how to present the truths of the Word of God in public, and how to do house-to-house work. The business affairs of the farm are to be wisely and carefully managed. {2MR 69.2}

Each student is to take himself in hand, and with God's help overcome the faults that mar his character.--Letter 215, 1904, pp. 3-6. (To M. A. Davis, June 30, 1904.) {2MR 69.3}

November 30, 1904

The condition of the Industrial School established for the training of Christian workers at Huntsville, Ala., appealed strongly to my sympathies. The large farm of three hundred and sixty acres, purchased by the General Conference as a home for this institution, will, with intelligent cultivation, meet a considerable portion of the running expenses of the school. But the buildings have been inadequate for the work that should be done. The teachers and students have very few schoolroom appliances. In the students' home and on the farm there have been very few suitable facilities. Some new buildings must be erected and furnished. Good bathrooms are greatly needed. In connection with this school, students are to be trained for the medical missionary work. {PCO 62.3}

1905

In God's plan for Israel every family had a home on the land, with sufficient ground for tilling. Thus were provided both the means and the incentive for a useful, industrious, and self-supporting life. And no devising of men has ever improved upon that plan. To the world's departure from it is owing, to a large degree, the poverty and wretchedness that exist today. {MH 183.3}

At the settlement of Israel in Canaan, the land was divided

among the whole people, the Levites only, as ministers of the sanctuary, being excepted from the equal distribution. The tribes were numbered by families, and to each family, according to its numbers, was apportioned an inheritance. {MH 184.1}

And although one might for a time dispose of his possession, he could not permanently barter away the inheritance of his children. When able to redeem his land, he was at liberty at any time to do so. Debts were remitted every seventh year, and in the fiftieth, or year of jubilee, all landed property reverted to the original owner. {MH 184.2}

"The land shall not be sold forever," was the Lord's direction; "for the land is Mine; for ye are strangers and sojourners with Me. And in all the land of your possession ye shall grant a redemption for the land. If thy brother be waxen poor, and hath sold away some of his possession, and if any of his kin come to redeem it, then shall he redeem that which his brother sold. And if the man . . . himself be able to redeem it; . . . he may return unto his possession. But if he be not able to restore it to him, then that which is sold shall remain in the hand of him that hath bought it until the year of jubilee." Leviticus 25:23-28. {MH 184.3}

"Ye shall hallow the fiftieth year, and proclaim liberty throughout all the land unto all the inhabitants thereof: it shall be a jubilee unto you; and ye shall return every man unto his possession, and ye shall return every man unto his family." Verse 10. {MH 185.1}

Thus every family was secured in its possession, and a safeguard was afforded against the extremes of either wealth or want. {MH 185.2}

The plan of life that God gave to Israel was intended as an object lesson for all mankind. If these principles were carried out today, what a different place this world would be! {MH 188.4}

Within the vast boundaries of nature there is still room for the suffering and needy to find a home. Within her bosom there are resources sufficient to provide them with food. Hidden in the depths of the earth are blessings for all who have courage and will and perseverance to gather her treasures. {MH 188.5}

The tilling of the soil, the employment that God appointed to man in Eden, opens a field in which there is opportunity for multitudes to gain a subsistence.

"Trust in the Lord, and do good;
So shalt thou dwell in the land, and verily thou
shalt be fed." Psalm 37:3. {MH 189.1}

Thousands and tens of thousands might be working upon the soil who are crowded into the cities, watching for a chance to earn a trifle. In many cases this trifle is not spent for bread, but is put into the till of the liquor seller, to obtain that which destroys soul and body. {MH 189.2}

Many look upon labor as drudgery, and they try to obtain a livelihood by scheming rather than by honest toil. This desire to get a living without work opens the door to wretchedness and vice and crime almost without limit. {MH 189.3}

Christian farmers can do real missionary work in helping the poor to find homes on the land, and in teaching them how to till the soil and make it productive. Teach them how to use the implements of agriculture, how to cultivate various crops, how to plant and care for orchards. {MH 193.2}

Many who till the soil fail to secure adequate returns because of their neglect. Their orchards are not properly cared for, the crops are not put in at the right time, and a mere surface work is done in cultivating the soil. Their ill success they charge to the unproductiveness of the land. False witness is often borne in condemning land that, if properly worked, would yield rich returns. The narrow plans, the little strength put forth, the little study as to the best methods, call loudly for reform. {MH 193.3}

Let proper methods be taught to all who are willing to learn. If any do not wish you to speak to them of advanced ideas, let the lessons be given silently. Keep up the culture of your own land. Drop a word to your neighbors when you can, and let the harvest be eloquent in favor of right methods. Demonstrate what can be done with the land when properly worked. {MH 193.4}

Missionary families are needed to settle in the waste places. Let farmers, financiers, builders, and those who are skilled in various arts and crafts, go to neglected fields, to improve the land, to establish industries, to prepare humble homes for themselves, and to help their neighbors. {MH 194.3}

If all were done that could be done in providing homes in families for orphan children, there would still remain very many requiring care. Many of them have received an inheritance of evil. They are unpromising, unattractive, perverse, but they are the purchase of the blood of Christ, and in His sight are just as precious as are our own little ones. Unless a helping hand is held out to them, they will grow up in ignorance and drift into vice and crime. Many of these children could be rescued through the work of orphan asylums. {MH 205.3}

Such institutions, to be most effective, should be modeled as closely as possible after the plan of a Christian home. Instead of large establishments, bringing great numbers together, let there be small institutions in different places. Instead of being in or near some town or large city, they should be in the country where land can be secured for cultivation and the children can be brought into contact with nature and can have the benefits of industrial training. {MH 205.4}

Plans should be devised for keeping patients out of doors. For those who are able to work, let some pleasant, easy employment be provided. Show them how agreeable and helpful this outdoor work is. Encourage them to breathe the fresh air. Teach them to breathe deeply, and in breathing and speaking to exercise the abdominal muscles. This is an education that will be invaluable to them. {MH 264.4}

Exercise in the open air should be prescribed as a life-giving necessity. And for such exercises there is nothing better than the cultivation of the soil. Let patients have flower beds to care for, or work to do in the orchard or vegetable garden. As they are encouraged to leave their rooms and spend time in the open air, cultivating flowers or doing some other light, pleasant work, their attention will be diverted from themselves and their sufferings. {MH 265.1}

The more the patient can be kept out of doors, the less care will he require. The more cheerful his surroundings, the more helpful will he be. Shut up in the house, be it ever so elegantly furnished, he will grow fretful and gloomy. Surround him with the beautiful things of nature; place him where he can see the flowers growing and hear the birds singing, and his heart will break into song in harmony with the songs of the birds. Relief will come to body and mind. The intellect will be awakened, the imagination quickened, and the mind prepared to appreciate the beauty of God's word. {MH 265.2}

January 10, 1905

To those assembled in council at Nashville, Dear Brethren, {PCO 104.4}

I am deeply interested in the work that is being done in the Southern field, and especially in the work of the Huntsville School. This school farm was represented to me as having on it fruit trees in full bearing, and also a variety of grains and vegetables, which were in a flourishing condition. Then the words were spoken: "This land is a precious treasure. If thoroughly cultivated, it will yield a valuable increase for the support of the school. But special pains must be taken in its cultivation. Much more may be realized from it than now appears possible. If properly treated, this land will be a lesson book to the students, and to our people, and to those not of our faith." {PCO 104.5}

There was presented before me a gathering in of the harvest with much rejoicing. Painstaking effort had gained a liberal reward. Then the explanation was given: "Thus it may be in the lives of the students, if they will put forth patient effort to acquire knowledge and will respond to the painstaking effort put forth in their behalf. The seed sown by the diligent efforts of the teachers will be seen in the development of valuable faculties, which will be of use in the Lord's cause. The students will gain knowledge that they can give to their own race." {PCO 104.6}

When I was last in Nashville, I was asked whether it would not be best to dispose of the Huntsville School Farm and purchase land elsewhere. Those who asked this question thought that perhaps there was more land in this farm than could be properly managed by the students. {PCO 105.1}

When I was on the steamer Morning Star, the matter was opened before me. I wrote out the instruction given and read it to a large number at the Huntsville meeting. I will have this matter copied and sent to Brother Rogers and to other workers in the South. {PCO 105.2}

Note: The instruction she received on the Morning Star was written out on June 10, 1904. Portions of this instruction are found in the preceding pages.

March 30, 1905

From San Diego we returned to Los Angeles, and on Tuesday, December 6, we went to Redlands for a few days' visit. A little way out from Los Angeles, the scenery became very uninteresting. We passed through much barren land. Here and there, the desert, by means of irrigation, had been converted into flourishing orange groves; but for miles and miles at a stretch the land was uncultivated. As we rode along, I remembered scenes presented to me years before, of barren land, such as that through which we were passing, being cultivated and improved, and, by irrigation, made to yield rich returns. I was instructed that this was an object-lesson of the influence that the saving grace of Christ should have upon the hearts and lives of human beings. And had those to whom God has given the riches of the water of life, realized the responsibilities resting upon them as stewards of the grace of God, and gone forth as faithful missionaries into all the barren places of the earth, the wilderness would have been made to blossom as the garden of the Lord. {RH, March 30, 1905 par. 1}

As we neared Redlands, the aspect of the country changed entirely. Cultivation and irrigation have transformed the desert into beautiful and fertile orange groves, which, at the time of our visit, were laden with fruit. On reaching Redlands, we went to the home of Brother and Sister E. S. Ballenger, where we were entertained during our stay. {RH, March 30, 1905 par. 8}

April 14, 1905

Dear Brethren and Sisters: I ask you, What are you doing as individuals, to benefit the colored people? Are you engaged in personal missionary work? As a church, what are you doing to provide a suitable sanitarium for the colored race? {4MR 26.4}

In the night season, I received counsel from One who never errs. I heard some who spoke in favor of purchasing the dark, unhealthful place now used as a sanitarium, putting in some improvements, and continuing the work in the same place. Decided instruction was given: {4MR 27.1}

"You are not to carry out the plans you contemplate. The present situation of the colored sanitarium is very objectionable. Let some place be secured where there is plenty of sunlight, and where there is land to raise fruit and vegetables. Let the sanitarium be moved to a suitable location, and so equipped that the better class of colored people may be accommodated, and may be favorably impressed." {4MR 27.2}

For some time I have considered that the place which J. E. White left, Edgefield Junction, near Madison, Tennessee, is the proper place for the establishment of a colored sanitarium. I hope that our brethren will see the necessity of making this move for it is sensible, merciful, and consistent. The present showing of neglect of the colored people must be changed. {4MR 27.3}

The fact that someone of our brethren is located on or near the property is not a sufficient excuse for not securing it for a colored sanitarium. For anyone to urge merely a personal consideration against such a move is a sign of selfishness, and shows a disregard of the Lord's plans. Far better would it be to repay what such a one had invested than to permit the enterprise to be blocked by such an excuse. {4MR 27.4}

Will our brethren and sisters in Nashville consider that they are being tested and tried? Some who have neglected to do the work that should have been done long ago, are in heaven accounted as unfaithful stewards. A more decided interest should be manifested in the work of helping the colored people. {4MR 27.5}

If in the future we are to do nothing more for the colored people than we have done in the past, let us lay aside all pretense that we have entered Nashville for the purpose of helping them. If the interest we have taken in helping those who are laboring in the South is to have no better results, we had better turn our attention to the opening of the work in new fields, until the converting power of God comes upon the church in Nashville, and barriers are removed.

The Lord is not pleased with the present showing. Let there now be a reformation, and the Lord will work with those who are willing to cooperate with Him. {4MR 28.1}

The men whom God has called to act a part in the work in the Southern field need closely to examine themselves in the light of God's word. From the example of Christ they need to learn to manifest kindness and tender sympathy for those who are afflicted, or who are laboring in hard and trying places. Those who are connected with the work of God should be ministers of healing.-- Letter 119, 1905, pp. 1-3. (To the members of the Nashville Church, April 14, 1905.) {4MR 28.2}

July, 1905

The character of the buildings, the terraced hill, covered by graceful pepper trees, the profusion of flowers and shrubs, the tall shade trees, the orchards and fields,--all combine to make this place meet fully the descriptions that I have given in the past of the place presented to me as the most perfect for sanitarium work. Everything at Loma Linda is fresh and wholesome and attractive. The patients could live out of doors a large part of the time. The land will serve as a school for the education of patients. By out-door exercises and working in the soil, men and women will regain their health. Rational methods for the cure of disease will be used in a variety of ways. Drugs will be discarded. {LLM 110.3}

Out of the cities, has been my constant advice. But it has taken years for our people to become aroused to an understanding of the situation. It has taken years for them to realize that the Lord would have them leave the cities and do their work in the quiet of the country, away from the turmoil and noise and confusion. We are thankful to God for Loma Linda. It is one of the best locations for sanitarium work that I have ever seen. At this place the sick can be given every natural advantage for regaining health and strength. {LLM 110.4}

September 23, 1905

We need a genuine education in the art of cooking. Instead of multiplying our restaurants, it will be better to form classes, where you may teach the people how to make good bread, and how to put together the ingredients to make healthful food combinations from the grains and the vegetables. Such an education will assist in creating a desire among our people to move out of the cities, to secure land in the country, where they can raise their own fruit and vegetables. Then they can care for their gardens, and their food will not come to them half spoiled and decayed. {8MR 173.1}

Note: Extracted from a talked given on restaurant work.

October 18, 1905

At one time I hoped that our brethren connected with our medical work in Nashville could see their way clear to establish a sanitarium on a part of the Madison school farm. Instruction has been given me that with our large schools there should be connected small sanitariums, that the students may have opportunity to gain a knowledge of medical missionary work. This line of work is to be brought into our schools as a part of the regular instruction. {SpTB18 23.1}

The Madison school should have a small sanitarium of its own, [THE SMALL SANITARIUM HERE CALLED FOR, HAS SINCE BEEN ESTABLISHED.] that the students may have opportunity to learn how to give the simple treatments. This is the plan that we have been directed to follow. And if the brethren connected with the medical work in Nashville could have seen their way clear to locate the sanitarium on the school farm near enough the school for there to be co-operation between the two institutions and far enough from it to prevent one from interfering with the work of the other, I should have been glad. I have thought much of these things in connection with the Nashville Sanitarium, and of the advantages to be gained if the school and the sanitarium could be near enough together to blend their work. But I have received no positive instruction regarding the exact location of the Nashville Sanitarium, and in this particular case I can not speak in decided terms. I dare not take the responsibility of saying anything to change the present arrangements. {SpTB18 23.2}

In order for the best results to be secured by the establishment of a sanitarium on the school farm, there would need to be perfect harmony between the workers of the institution. But this might be difficult to secure. . . . Both those at the head of the sanitarium and those at the head of the school would need to guard against clinging tenaciously to ideas of their own regarding things that are really non-essentials. {SpTB18 24.1}

May 10, 1906

We have your recent letter. I need not wait for reflection before saying that I believe the best plan is that of first strengthening the work in Adelaide. The climate is more healthful, and the spiritual atmosphere much more favorable than that of Melbourne. This is the way that the matter has been presented to me, but I hoped you would decide the matter from your own judgment. I believe that after placing the whole matter before the Lord, the brethren will come to a harmonious decision. The Lord understands all our necessities. {21MR 90.1}

The outlook for establishing a sanitarium at Adelaide is much more favorable than the outlook for establishing one at Melbourne. The city of Melbourne is not the place to establish a sanitarium. It has been plainly presented to me that the sanitarium which you are planning to establish should be located in the most healthful place you can secure. But my warning is that of the angel who, standing in Melbourne, said in a clear, distinct voice, Establish not schools or sanitariums in the cities. In the future, cities will certainly feel the terrible results of earthquakes and fires. Cities will be destroyed by flood and by lightnings. Out of the cities, is my message at this time. {21MR 90.2}

Be assured that the call is for our people to locate miles away from the large cities. One look at San Francisco as it is today would speak to your intelligent minds, showing you the necessity of getting out of the cities. Do not establish institutions in the cities, but seek a rural location. The call is, "Come out from among them, and be ye separate." The very atmosphere of the city is polluted. Let your schools be established away from the cities, where agricultural and other industries can be carried on. {21MR 90.3}

The Lord calls for His people to locate away from the cities, for in such an hour as ye think not, fire and brimstone will be rained from heaven upon these cities. Proportionate to their sins will be their visitation. When one city is destroyed, let not our people regard this matter as a light affair, and think that they may, if favorable opportunity offers, build themselves homes in that same destroyed city. {21MR 90.4}

Note: This letter, written to Dr. Kress in Australia, came just less than a month after the great 1906 earthquake in San Francisco. The quake occurred just after 5am on April 18 and when combined with the ensuing fire, destroyed 80% of the city. It is this which Ellen White is referring to when she speaks of seeing San Francisco "as it is today." Though she was in Los Angeles at the time of the earthquake she would return to her home in northern California via San Francisco two weeks later.

September 19, 1906

Since daylight I have written eleven pages in regard to the manufacture and sale of flake foods on the Pacific Coast. Dr. Kellogg and his brother offer to sell for forty-five thousand dollars, the right to manufacture and sell corn flakes in a certain section. The light given me is that we are not to accept this offer. Neither the territory nor the knowledge regarding health foods belongs to Dr. Kellogg. This is the Lord's talent. He has not made it over to any man, to be handled as his own property and invention, and to speculate upon for his own benefit. It has not been given to any man to be used to oppress his fellow-men. {HFM 82.3}

"Thus speaketh the Lord of hosts, saying, Execute true judgment, and shew mercy and compassion every man to his brother; and oppress not the widow, nor the fatherless, the stranger, nor the poor; and let none of you imagine evil against his brother in your heart." Zechariah 7:9-10. {HFM 83.1}

The third and fourth chapters of Malachi teach many important lessons. They are full of weighty sentences. We are to consider these chapters carefully. The Lord is weighing character. Every chapter of the work carried on in Battle Creek has been recorded in the books of heaven, from the first action to the last. {HFM 83.2}

Our people are not to invest large sums of money in the production of health foods. It has been plainly stated that the light regarding health foods was not given for one man's benefit alone. I have been given light on this subject. We are not to accept this offer.

Our people can use the talent God has given them to prepare foods such as He would be pleased to have them prepare for the use of the common people. The Lord has given the sunshine and the rain, and has caused the fruit to grow, and the earth to produce that which may be prepared for the food of mankind. He requires His family diligently to till the soil, that it may produce those things that may be used as food. They are to plant the seed, and care for it as it grows. This is the provision that He has made for man's food. He has given genius and tact to man, that he may prepare from the fruit of the earth a great variety of foods. Grains, vegetables, and fruits are to be planted and cultivated. The ground is to be dressed and worked, and the earth will produce her treasures. . . . {HFM 83.3}

Men and women are to be taught how to prepare food for the common people. This branch of education is to be given a place in every school established. The students are to be patiently taught how to cook, as well as how to read. The very best methods are to be employed in teaching the industries essential to everyday life. Instruction is to be faithfully given in simple methods of treating the sick. {HFM 84.1}

The Lord has given to us as a people great knowledge upon health reform. The work is to go forward. But God forbid that the food business should continue to take so large a place as it has taken. The capabilities and talents of valuable workers are not to be confined to the production of foods, while spiritual interests become secondary. This is a matter that must be dealt with upon a right basis, else it will become a great hindrance to us in our work of soul-saving. -Letter 354, 1906. Written September 19, 1906. {HFM 84.2}

June 18, 1907

God has revealed to me that we are in positive danger of bringing into our educational work the customs and fashions that prevail in the schools of the world. If teachers are not guarded in their work, they will place on the necks of their students worldly yokes instead of the yoke of Christ. The plan of the schools we shall establish in these closing years of the work is to be of an entirely different order from those we have instituted in the past. {SpTB11 28.1}

For this reason, God bids us establish schools away from the cities, where, without let or hindrance, we can carry on the work of education upon plans that are in harmony with the solemn message that is committed to us for the world. Such an education as this can best be worked out where there is land to cultivate, and where the physical exercise taken by the students can be of such a nature as to act a valuable part in their character- building, and to fit them for usefulness in the fields to which they shall go. {SpTB11 28.2}

God will bless the work of those schools that are conducted according to His design. When we were laboring to establish the educational work in Australia, the Lord revealed to us that this school must not pattern after any schools that had been established in the past. This was to be a sample school. The school was organized on the plan that God had given us, and He has prospered its work. {SpTB11 28.3}

I have been shown that in our educational work we are not to follow the methods that have been adopted in our older established schools. There is among us too much clinging to old customs, and because of this we are far behind where we should be in the development of the third angel's message. Because men could not comprehend the purpose of God in the plans laid before us for the education of the workers, methods have been followed in some of our schools which have retarded rather than advanced the work of God. Years have passed into eternity with small results that might have shown the accomplishment of a great work. If the Lord's will had been done by the workers in earth as the angels do it in heaven, much that now remains to be done, would be already accomplished, and noble results would be seen as the fruit of missionary effort. {SpTB11 29.1}

The usefulness learned on the school farm is the very education that is most essential for those who go out as missionaries to many foreign fields. If this training is given with the glory of God in view, great results will be seen. No work will be more effectual than that done by those who, having obtained an education in practical life, go forth to mission fields with the message of truth, prepared to instruct as they have been instructed. The knowledge they have obtained in the tilling of the soil and other lines of manual work, and which they carry with them to their fields of labor, will make them a blessing even in heathen lands. {SpTB11 29.2}

Before we can carry the message of present truth in all its fullness to other countries, we must first break every yoke. We must come into the line of true education, walking in the wisdom of God, and not in the wisdom of the world. God calls for messengers who will be true reformers. We must educate, educate, to prepare a people who will understand the message, and then give the message to the world. {SpTB11 30.1}

September 10, 1907

At the Huntsville School [Oakwood] a thorough work is to be done in training men to cultivate the soil and to grow fruits and vegetables. Let no one despise this work. Agriculture is the ABC of industrial education. Let the erection of the buildings for the school and the sanitarium be an education to the students. Help the teachers to understand that their perceptions must be clear, their actions in harmony with the truth, for it is only when they stand in right relation to God that they will be able to work out His plan for themselves and for the souls with whom, as instructors, they are brought in contact. {PCO 45.2}

October 22, 1907

I received your letter giving the particulars regarding your grounds and the cultivation of certain lines of fruit. While we were in Australia, we adopted the very plan you speak of--digging deep trenches and filling them in with dressing that would create good soil. This we did in the cultivation of tomatoes, oranges, lemons, peaches, and grapes. {15MR 54.2}

The man of whom we purchased our peach trees told me that he would be pleased to have me observe the way they were planted. I then asked him to let me show him how it had been represented in the night season that they should be planted. I ordered my hired man to dig a deep cavity in the ground, then put in rich dirt, then stones, then rich dirt. After this he put in layers of earth and dressing until the hole was filled. I told the nurseryman that I had planted in this way in the rocky soil in America. I invited him to visit me when these fruits should be ripe. He said to me, "You need no lesson from me to teach you how to plant the trees." {15MR 54.3}

Our crops were very successful. The peaches were the most

beautiful in coloring, and the most delicious in flavor of any that I had tasted. We grew the large yellow Crawford and other varieties, grapes, apricots, nectarines, and plums. {15MR 54.4}

A member of parliament who came to Cooranbong occasionally, and who had purchased the house in which we first lived in Cooranbong, visited our garden and orchard, and was greatly pleased with it. Several times we filled a large basket with fruit and took it to him and his wife at their home, and they were profuse in their thanks. After this they would always recognize us on the cars, and speak of the great treat they had had in the fruit from our orchard. When they would visit us at our farm, they were always at liberty to eat all they wanted from the garden, and usually carried away a basket of fruit to their home. {15MR 55.1}

These favors brought us returns in several ways. Mention was made in the papers of the work being done by the students on the Avondale estate. And years afterward, when the terrible drought came, and the cattle were dying for want of pasture and food, the papers spoke of the wonderful exception to the drought to be found on the Avondale tract of land. They compared it to an oasis in the desert. Our crops were not cut off, and the farm flourished remarkably, notwithstanding the lack of rain. {15MR 55.2}

When we were investigating the land at Cooranbong, our brethren held off from purchasing for a whole year, thinking to find in some other locality land that would compare well with the rich soil of Iowa. This they finally decided could not be found. But the work was hindered for a whole year because some of the brethren had not the faith to move forward in spite of the discouraging appearances. {15MR 55.3}

In the night season a representation had been given me that revealed this lack of faith. I seemed to be on the Avondale land, and while the horses were breaking away through the forest, I walked in an open space close to where our school buildings now stand. I saw a furrow made in the soil one foot deep and about four in length. Two of the brethren stood at the furrow, one at each end; they were examining the soil, and declaring it to be of no value. But one stood by who said, "You have misjudged the worth of this land." He then explained the value of the different strata in the soil and their uses. {15MR 55.4}

When we came to Avondale to examine the estate, I went with the brethren to the tract of land. After a time we came to the place I had dreamed of, and there was the furrow that I had seen. The brethren looked at it in surprise. How had it come there, they asked. Then I told them the dream that I had had. "Well," they replied, "you can see that the soil is not good." "That," I answered, "was the testimony borne by the men in my dream, and that was given as the reason why we should not occupy the land. But one stood upon the upturned furrow, and said, 'False testimony has been borne concerning this soil. God can furnish a table in the wilderness.'" {15MR 56.1}

The fifteen hundred acres were purchased. The marshland had to have considerable attention in order to drain off the water. But when this was done, even this part was found to be valuable. The crops that the land yielded proved the truth of the words of the Messenger. But the lack of faith that was manifested in taking up the work cost us the loss of time and means. {15MR 56.2}

The Lord knows what is best for His work. That which was, as it were, a hiding place in the wilderness has proved to be a profitable tract of land. And we have learned that if we would have a rich experience in our Christian life, we must let the Lord direct. {15MR 56.3}

October 24, 1907

Those who go forth from our schools to engage in mission work will have need of an experience in the cultivation of the soil and in other lines of manual labor. They should receive a training that will fit them to take hold of any line of work in the fields to which they shall be called. No work will be more effectual than that done by those who, having obtained an education in practical life, go forth prepared to instruct as they have been instructed. {RH, October 24, 1907 par. 3}

In his teachings the Saviour represented the world as a vineyard. We would do well to study the parables in which this figure is used. If in our schools the land were more faithfully cultivated, the buildings more disinterestedly cared for by the students, the love of sports and amusements, which causes so much perplexity in our school work, would pass away. {RH, October 24, 1907 par. 4}

When the Lord placed our first parents in the garden of Eden, it was with the injunction that they "dress it" and "keep it." God had finished his work of creation, and had pronounced all things very good. Everything was adapted to the end for which it was made. While Adam and Eve obeyed God, their labors in the garden were a pleasure; the earth yielded of its abundance for their wants. But when man departed from his obedience to God, he was doomed to wrestle with the seeds of Satan's sowing, and to earn his bread by the sweat of his brow. Henceforth he must battle in toil and hardship against the power to which he had yielded his will. {RH, October 24, 1907 par. 5}

It was God's purpose to remove by toil the evil which man brought into the world by disobedience. By toil the temptations of Satan might be made ineffectual, and the tide of evil be stayed. The Son of God was given to the world, by his death to make atonement for the sins of the world, by his life to teach men how the plans of the enemy were to be thwarted. Taking upon himself the nature of man, Christ entered into the sympathies and interests of his brethren, and by a life of untiring labor taught how men might become laborers together with God in the building up of his kingdom in the world. {RH, October 24, 1907 par. 6}

If those who have received instruction concerning God's plan for the education of the youth in these last days, will surrender their wills to God, he will teach them his will and his way. Christ is to be the teacher in all our schools. If teachers and students will give him his rightful place, he will work through them to carry out the plan of redemption. {RH, October 24, 1907 par. 7}

January 6, 1908

The Lord selected the farm at Madison, and He signified that it should be worked on right lines, that others, learning from the workers in Madison, might take up a similar work and conduct it in a like manner. Brethren Sutherland and Magan are chosen of God and faithful, and the Lord of heaven says of them, I have a work for these men to do in Madison, a special work in educating and training young men and women for missionary fields. The Spirit of the Lord is with His workers. He has not restricted the labors of these self-denying, self-sacrificing men. {20MR 100.2}

The school at Madison not only educates in a knowledge of the Scriptures, but it gives a practical training that fits the student to go forth as a self-supporting missionary to the field to which he is called. In his student days he is taught how to build, simply and substantially, how to cultivate the land and care for the stock. All these lines are of great educational value. To this is added the knowledge of how to treat the sick and care for the injured. This training for medical missionary work is one of the grandest objects for which any school can be established. There are many suffering from disease and injuries who, when relieved of pain, will be prepared to listen to the truth. Our Saviour was a mighty healer. In His name there may be many miracles wrought in the South and in other conferences, through the instrumentality of the trained medical missionary. Therefore, centers for training must be formed. {20MR 100.3}

The class of education given at the Madison school is such as will be accounted a treasure of great value by those who take up missionary work in foreign fields. My brethren, let no hindrance be placed in the way of men and women who are seeking to gain such an education as those at the Madison school are receiving. They are working after the Lord's directions. If many more in other schools were receiving a similar training, we as a people would become a spectacle to the world, to angels, and to men. The message should quickly be carried to every country, and souls now in darkness would be brought to the light. These men under the special light the Lord has given are not to be hindered in any way, for the Lord is leading them. {20MR 100.4}

It would have been pleasing to God if, while the Madison school has been doing its work, similar schools had been established in different parts of the Southern field. No soul should be left in darkness if by any possible means he can be enlightened. {20MR 100.5}

There is plenty of land lying waste in the South that might have been improved as the land about the Madison school has been improved. The time is soon coming when God's people, because of persecution, will be scattered in many countries. Those who have received an all-round education will have the advantage wherever they are. The Lord reveals divine wisdom in thus leading His people to the training of all their faculties and capabilities for the work of disseminating truth. {20MR 101.1}

Note: Written "To Those Bearing Responsibilities in Washington and Other Centers," January 6, 1908.

May 26, 1908

The Lord has given to the Southern field object lessons of different kinds. The education being given to the students at Madison, which trains the youth to build, to cultivate the land, and to care for cattle and poultry, will be of great advantage to them in the future. There is no better way of keeping the body in health than to follow the plan of training that the Madison school is carrying out. This is the same kind of work as we were instructed to do when we purchased the land for our school in Australia. The students had their hours for study and their hours for work on the land. They were taught to fell trees, to plant orchards, to cultivate the soil, and to erect buildings, and this training was a blessing to all who engaged in it. {11MR 181.3}

The Lord in His providence has brought about the establishment of the Madison school through the efforts of Brethren [E. A.] Sutherland and [P. T.] Magan, and a few faithful associates. Their labors have been performed under no ordinary circumstances. These men had an experience at Berrien Springs which was a severe one, but the Lord brought them safely through it and made it a means of blessing to them. They felt that they must go to the South and labor for this needy field. They went out not knowing whither they were going, and the Lord guided them to Madison, a beautiful place of 400 acres. For a time the way for the establishment of the work seemed hedged up. The Lord led His servants through a trying experience, but He saw the end from the beginning. When some of their brethren expostulated and labored to discourage them, the Lord encouraged. And the results of the efforts put forth at that place we can see; The Lord's blessing has rested upon their efforts. {11MR 182.1}

The work that the laborers have accomplished at Madison has done more to give a correct knowledge of what an all-round education means than any other school that has been established by Seventh-day Adventists in America. The Lord has given these teachers in the South an education that is of highest value, and it is a training that God would be pleased to have all our youth receive. {11MR 182.2}

The close confinement of students to mental work has cost the life of many precious youth. The Madison school, in its system of education, is showing that mental and physical powers, brain and muscle, must be equally taxed. The example that it has given in this respect is one that it would be well for all who engage in school work to emulate. If the physical and mental powers were equally taxed, there would be in our world far less of corruption of mind and far less feebleness of health.--Letter 168, 1908, pp. 3, 4. (To J. E. White and wife, May 26, 1908.) {11MR 182.3}

May 28, 1908

God has originated and proclaimed the principles on which divine and human agencies are to combine in temporal matters as well as all spiritual achievements. They are to be linked together in all human pursuits, in mechanical and agricultural labor, in mercantile and scientific enterprises. In all lines of work it is necessary that there be co-operation between God and man. God has provided facilities with which to enrich and beautify the earth. But the strength and ingenuity of human agencies are required to make the very best use of the material. God had filled the earth with treasure, but the gold and silver are hidden in the earth, and the exercise of man's powers is required to secure this treasure which God has provided. Man's energy and tact are to be used in connection with the power of God in bringing the gold and silver from the mines, and trees from the forest. But unless by his miracle-working power God co-operated with man, enabling him to use his physical and mental capabilities, the treasures in our world would be useless. {RH, May 28, 1908 par. 2}

We cannot keep ourselves for one moment. "We are kept by the power of God through faith unto salvation." We are utterly dependent upon God every moment of our lives. {RH, May 28, 1908 par. 3}

God desires every human being in our world to be a worker together with him. This is the lesson we are to learn from all useful employment, making homes in the forest, felling trees to build houses, clearing land for cultivation. God has provided the wood and the land, and to man he has given the work of putting them in such shape that they will be a blessing. In this work man is wholly dependent upon God. The fitting of the ships that cross the broad ocean is not alone due to the talent and ingenuity of the human agent. God is the great Architect. Without his co-operation, without the aid of the higher intelligences, how worthless would be the plans of men. God must aid, else every device is worthless. {RH, May 28, 1908 par. 4}

The human organism is the handiwork of God. The organs employed in all the different functions of the body were made by him. The Lord gives us food and drink, that the wants of the body may be supplied. He has given the earth different properties adapted to the growth of food for his children. He gives the sunshine and the showers, the early and the latter rain. He forms the clouds and sends the dew. All are his gifts. He has bestowed his blessings upon us liberally. But all these blessings will not restore in us his moral image, unless we co-operate with him, making painstaking effort to know ourselves, to understand how to care for the delicate human machinery. Man must diligently help to keep himself in harmony with nature's laws. He who co-operates with God in the work of keeping this wonderful machinery in order, who consecrates all his powers to God, seeking intelligently to obey the laws of nature, stands in his God-given manhood, and is recorded in the books of heaven as a man. {RH, May 28, 1908 par. 5}

God has given man land to be cultivated. But in order that the harvest may be reaped, there must be harmonious action between divine and human agencies. The plow and other implements of labor must be used at the right time. The seed must be sown in its season. Man is not to fail of doing his part. If he is careless and negligent, his unfaithfulness testifies against him. The harvest is proportionate to the energy he has expended. {RH, May 28, 1908 par. 6}

So it is in spiritual things. We are to be laborers together with God. Man is to work out his own salvation with fear and trembling, for it is God that worketh in him, both to will and to do of his good pleasure. There is to be co-partnership, a divine relation, between the Son of God and the repentant sinner. We are made sons and daughters of God. "As many as received him, to them gave he power to become the sons of God." Christ provides the mercy and grace so abundantly given to all who believe in him. He fulfils the terms upon which salvation rests. But we must act our part by accepting the blessing in faith. God works and man works. Resistance of temptation must come from man, who must draw his power from God. Thus he becomes a co-partner with Christ. {RH, May 28, 1908 par. 7}

1909 – The College of Medical Evangelists Founded (Loma Linda)

The Loma Linda Years (1909-1915)

January 13, 1909

There has been some delay in getting the title to the Buena Vista property [Sonoma, California]. We are looking forward to having the matter settled soon. This is an excellent site for a school. As soon as I saw it, I was sure that it would make an ideal place for the carrying on of our educational work, for we can combine physical work on the farm with the study of books. Here the students can be taught to build and to engage in many useful lines of labor, as the students at Madison are being taught to do. There should also be sanitarium facilities in connection with the school, for I have been shown that where we have a training school we should have a sanitarium where the students can receive instruction in caring for the sick and suffering.--Letter 18, 1909, p. 2. (To J. E. White and wife, Jan. 13, 1909.)

Note: In the early 1900's there was a desire to move Healdsburg College (PUC) to another location. During this time many different properties were visited, the Buena Vista property (near Sonoma) being one of them, was under serious consideration. Property near Angwin was eventually selected and is the current location of Pacific Union College.

February 6, 1909

For some time we have been deeply interested in the matter of securing a place for our school where we might find the very things we need in order that our educational interests may be advanced in right lines. {1MR 333.3}

With some of the brethren, I have looked at several locations. At one place, there was a large berry patch that yielded abundantly, but there was little land that could be cultivated. This was not a place suitable for our school. Our school should be located where the students can receive an education broader than that which the mere study of books will give. They must have such a training as will fit them for acceptable service if they are called to do pioneer work in mission fields either in America or in foreign countries. There must be land enough to give an experience in the cultivation of the soil, and to help largely in making the institution self supporting. {1MR 333.4}

Last spring some of us drove up into Lake County, and I looked carefully along the way, but saw nothing that was desirable as a location for our college. {1MR 334.1}

On our return from Southern California last September, we were asked by some of our brethren to look at some places near Sonoma. From the station we were driven in carriages to a place where there were two large houses situated in the midst of a very large orchard. I told the brethren that this was not the place for which I was looking, and that we could not afford to occupy these houses for a school, even if they should be given to us. {1MR 334.2}

From there we went to the Buena Vista property, and were shown the beautiful house. We looked through the large rooms on the first and second floors, and were told that the rooms on the third floor were just the same. {1MR 334.3}

After leaving the house, we drove quickly over some portions of the land. Consideration of what I saw, and the description given of other parts of the property made it plain that here were many most precious advantages. It was away from the strong temptations of city life. There was abundance of land for cultivation, and the water advantages were very valuable. All through the mountains there were little valleys where families might locate and have a few acres of land for garden or orchard. The many pipes laid over the grounds made it possible to use water freely both for the buildings and for the land. {1MR 334.4}

April 29, 1909

We are endeavoring to bring the colored people to that place where they can be self-supporting. The time will come when you will be able to escape many of the evils that will come upon the world because you have obtained a correct knowledge of how to plant and to build, and how to carry on various enterprises. This is why we want this land occupied and cultivated, why we want buildings put up. The students are to learn how to plant and to build and to sow.

As they learn to do this, they will see a work before them which they will be very glad to have a part in. Opportunities will present themselves by which they can make themselves a blessing to those around them. {PCO 7.6}

"Is it not to deal thy bread to the hungry, and that thou bring the poor that are cast out to thy house? when thou seest the naked, that thou cover him; and that thou hide not thyself from thine own flesh?" It is the privilege of every student and worker upon this school land to know what it is to be moved by the impulse of the Spirit of God. {PCO 7.7}

"Then shall thy light break forth as the morning, and thine health shall spring forth speedily." Why this assurance regarding the health? Health is given because you learn to use your muscles as well as your brain powers. It is very important that we tax our physical and mental powers equally. "Thy righteousness shall go before thee," the Lord continues, "and the glory of the Lord shall be thy reward." How will our righteousness go before us? It will be revealed in righteous words, in righteous actions, in our useful employments. This work is given to the colored people as surely as it is given to the white people. According to their opportunities they are to work out faithfully the problems that God presents to them. When we do the work that God requires of us, the blessings He has promised will attend us. {PCO 8.1}

If we will do justice, if we will exalt the truth, the Lord Himself will be our Keeper and our Preserver, enabling us to do His will. God takes care of those who are looked down upon by their fellow men. It is because He regards the needs of those who are despised and rejected that we have this school farm where you can receive a preparation for labor right here in the South. It is His desire that those who receive a training here shall go forth to labor to lift up the oppressed, to strengthen the weak hands, that through your efforts men and women may learn to honor and glorify God. The teaching of this fifty-eighth chapter of Isaiah means just this to you. {PCO 8.2}

Note: The above is a portion of a talk give to the students at Oakwood on April 29, 1909.

May 7, 1909

We are to educate the youth to exercise equally the mental and the physical powers. The healthful exercise of the whole being will give an education that is broad and comprehensive. We had stern work to do in Australia in educating parents and youth along these lines; but we persevered in our efforts until the lesson was learned that in order to have an education that was complete, the time of study must be divided between the gaining of book knowledge and the securing of a knowledge of practical work. Part of each day was spent in useful work, the students learning how to clear the land, how to cultivate the soil, and how to build houses, using time that would otherwise have been spent in playing games and seeking amusement. And the Lord blessed the students who thus devoted their time to acquiring habits of usefulness. {RH, November 11, 1909 par. 19}

Instruct the students not to regard as most essential the theoretical part of their education. Let it be more and more deeply impressed upon every student that we should have an intelligent understanding of how to treat the physical system. And there are many who would have greater intelligence in these matters if they would not confine themselves to years of study without a practical experience. The more fully we put ourselves under the direction of God, the greater knowledge we shall receive from God. Let us say to our students: Keep yourselves in connection with the Source of all power. Ye are laborers together with God. He is to be our chief instructor. {RH, November 11, 1909 par. 20}

Note: The paragraphs above were are also found in the Spalding Magan collection where it is recorded that they were originally part of a letter written to the teachers at Union College on May 7, 1909.

January 29, 1910

The time has come when every advantage to be gained for the furtherance of the work should be recognized, for we need all the strength we can obtain. Christ is soon coming, and Satan knows that his time is short. As we draw near to the close of time the cities will become more and more corrupt, and more and more objectionable as places for establishing centers of our work. The dangers of travel will increase, confusion and drunkenness will abound. If there can be found places in retired mountain regions where it would be difficult for the evils of the cities to enter, let our people secure such places for our sanitariums and advanced schools. The two institutions may be far enough apart so that there need be no confusion. {10MR 260.3}

Let parents understand that the training of their children is an important work in the saving of souls. In country places abundant useful exercise will be found in doing those things that need to be done, and which will give physical health by developing nerve and muscle. "Out of the cities" is my message for the education of our children. {10MR 260.4}

God gave to our first parents the means of true education when He instructed them to till the soil and care for their garden home. After sin came in, through disobedience to the Lord's requirements, the work to be done in cultivating the ground was greatly multiplied, for the earth, because of the curse, brought forth weeds and thistles. But the employment itself was not given because of sin. The great Master Himself blessed the work of tilling the soil. {10MR 261.1}

It is Satan's purpose to attract men and women to the cities, and to gain this object he invents every kind of novelty and amusement, every kind of excitement. And the cities of the earth today are becoming as were the cities before the Flood. {10MR 261.2}

August 29, 1911

"Loma Linda is an important center. We needed this place and all its advantages. We were successful in obtaining it, and we have had success in operating it, notwithstanding the opposition shown by some who should have been acting as helpers in the effort to equip a sanitarium properly. I have a deep interest in Loma Linda. It is a beautiful place. For sanitarium work, we could not have a more favorable situation. And it is well adapted for the other lines of work that we desire to see done there. {SpTB17b 18.1}

"Recently the question arose about securing more of the nearby land that is for sale. One piece, a tract of eighty-six acres, has already been purchased, and there is now on sale another tract of forty-seven acres joining the Loma Linda property. Because this piece of land is so near to our Loma Linda buildings, we do not want to see it sold to unbelievers, who will divide it up, and sell it to those who may desire to crowd into this neighborhood. In the night season I was talking to our brethren, telling them that this must not be allowed, and pointing out what unfavorable results would follow. If this piece of land should be purchased by unbelievers, and divided up and sold to those who would be no help to our work, the injury to Loma Linda would be serious and lasting. I cannot bear the thought of this. Cannot a group of individuals who are alive to the vital interests of the Lord's work, unite together and make this land our property? Then if we wish to sell a portion of it, let it be sold to our people. There is an orange orchard on the place, and this could be handled to advantage by the Sanitarium. The institution is hardly complete without the control of this orchard. {SpTB17b 18.2}

"As the number of patients and students increases, more land will be needed. Grape vines could be planted, thus making it possible for the institution to produce its grapes. {SpTB17b 19.1}

"Families and institutions should learn to do more in the cultivation and improvement of land. If people only knew the value of the products of the ground, which the earth brings forth in their season, more diligent efforts would be made to cultivate the soil. All should be acquainted with the special value of fruit and vegetables fresh from the orchard and garden. {SpTB17b 19.2}

"Will not some of our brethren who thus far have invested but little in Loma Linda, help the Lord's cause by assisting in the purchase of this piece of land? I place this matter before you, feeling sure that you will not allow the land to pass into the hands of unbelievers. We ought not to place ourselves where we shall become unfavorably associated with those who could make it hard for us if they chose to do so, and restrict us to certain limits. . {SpTB17b 19.3}

"We must have room to keep ourselves distinct as a Sabbath-keeping people. The Lord has given directions that we are to make provision which will prevent our being harassed and inconvenienced by having to crowd in with unbelievers. I wish I might make on your minds the impression that has been made on mine regarding this matter. {SpTB17b 19.4}

October 3, 1912
The essential lesson of contented industry in the necessary

duties of life is yet to be learned by many of Christ's followers. It requires more grace, more stern discipline of character, to work for God in the capacity of mechanic, merchant, lawyer, or farmer, carrying the precepts of Christianity into the ordinary business of life, than to labor as an acknowledged missionary in the open field. It requires a strong spiritual nerve to bring religion into the workshop and the business office, sanctifying the details of everyday life, and ordering every transaction according to the standard of God's word. But this is what the Lord requires. {RH, October 3, 1912 par. 18}

1913

The thought of the eternal life should be woven into all to which the Christian sets his hand. If the work performed is agricultural or mechanical in its nature, it may still be after the pattern of the heavenly. It is the privilege of the preceptors and teachers of our schools to reveal in all their work the leading of the Spirit of God. Through the grace of Christ every provision has been made for the perfecting of Christlike characters; and God is honored when His people, in all their social and business dealings, reveal the principles of heaven. {CT 58.1}

Provision should have been made in past generations for education upon a larger scale. In connection with the schools should have been agricultural and manufacturing establishments. There should also have been teachers of household labor. And a portion of the time each day should have been devoted to labor that the physical and mental powers might be equally exercised. If schools had been established on the plan we have mentioned, there would not now be so many unbalanced minds. . . . {CT 288.1}

A constant strain upon the brain while the muscles are inactive, enfeebles the nerves and gives to students an almost uncontrollable desire for change and exciting amusements. When they are released, after being confined to study several hours each day, they are nearly wild. Many have never been controlled at home. They have been left to follow inclination, and they think that the restraint of the hours of study is a severe tax upon them; and because they have nothing to do after study hours, Satan suggests sport and mischief for a change. Their influence over other students is demoralizing. . . . {CT 288.2}

Had there been agricultural and manufacturing establishments connected with our schools, and had competent teachers been employed to educate the youth in the different branches of study and labor, devoting a portion of each day to mental improvement and a portion to physical labor, there would now be a more elevated class of youth to come upon the stage of action, to have influence in molding society. Many of the youth graduated from such institutions would come forth with stability of character. They would have perseverance, fortitude, and courage to surmount obstacles, and such principles that they would not be swayed by a wrong influence however popular. {CT 288.3}

There should have been experienced teachers to give lessons to young ladies in the cooking department. Young girls should have been taught how to cut, make, and mend garments, and thus become educated for the practical duties of life. For young men, there should have been establishments where they could learn different trades, which would bring into exercise their muscles as well as their mental powers. {CT 289.1}

If the youth can have but a one-sided education, which is of the greater consequence, a knowledge of the sciences, with all the disadvantages to health and life, or a knowledge of labor for practical life? We unhesitatingly answer, The latter. If one must be neglected, let it be the study of books. {CT 289.2}

In establishing our schools out of the cities, we shall give the students an opportunity to train the muscles to work as well as the brain to think. Students should be taught how to plant, how to gather the harvest, how to build, how to become acceptable missionary workers in practical lines. By their knowledge of useful industries they will often be enabled to break down prejudice; often they will be able to make themselves so useful that the truth will be recommended by the knowledge they possess. {CT 309.2}

In our school in Australia we educated the youth along these lines, showing them that in order to have an education that is complete, they must divide their time between the gaining of book knowledge and the securing of a knowledge of practical work. Part of each day was spent in manual labor. Thus the students learned how to clear the land, to cultivate the soil, and to build houses; and these lines of work were largely carried on in time that would otherwise have been spent in playing games and seeking for amusement. The Lord blessed the students who devoted their hours to learning lessons of usefulness. To the managers and teachers of that school I was instructed to say: {CT 310.1}

"Various industries should be carried on in our schools. The industrial instruction given should include the keeping of accounts, carpentry, and all that is comprehended in farming. Preparation should be made for the teaching of blacksmithing, painting, shoemaking, and for cooking, baking, washing, mending, typewriting, and printing. Every power at our command is to be brought into this training work, that students may go forth well equipped for the duties of practical life. {CT 310.2}

"Students should be given a practical education in agriculture. This will be of inestimable value to many in their future work. The training to be obtained in felling trees and in tilling the soil, as well as in literary lines, is the education that our youth should seek to obtain. Agriculture will open resources for self-support. Other lines of work, adapted to different students, may also be carried on. But the cultivation of the land will bring a special blessing to the workers. We should so train the youth that they will love to engage in the cultivation of the soil. {CT 311.1}

Let the students who are engaged in building do their tasks with thoroughness, and let them learn from these tasks lessons that will help in their character building. In order to have perfect characters, they must make their work as perfect as possible. Into every line of labor let there be brought that stability which means true economy. If in our schools the land were more faithfully cultivated, the buildings more disinterestedly cared for by the students, the love of sports and amusements, which causes so much perplexity in our schoolwork, would pass away. {CT 312.1}

Skill in the common arts is a gift from God. He provides both the gift and wisdom to use the gift aright. When He desired a work done on the tabernacle He said, "See, I have called by name Bezaleel the son of Uri, the son of Hur, of the tribe of Judah: and I have filled him with the Spirit of God, in wisdom, and in understanding, and in knowledge, and in all manner of workmanship." Exodus 31:2, 3. Through the prophet Isaiah the Lord said, "Give ye ear, and hear My voice; hearken, and hear My speech. Doth the plowman plow all day to sow? doth he open and break the clods of his ground? When he hath made plain the face thereof, doth he not cast abroad the fitches, and scatter the cumin, and cast in the principal wheat and the appointed barley and the rye in their place? For his God doth instruct him to discretion, and doth teach him. {CT 314.1}

"For the fitches are not threshed with a threshing instrument, neither is a cart wheel turned about upon the cumin; but the fitches are beaten out with a staff, and the cumin with a rod. Bread corn is bruised; because he will not ever be threshing it, nor break it with the wheel of his cart, nor bruise it with his horsemen. This also cometh forth from the Lord of hosts, which is wonderful in counsel, and excellent in working." Isaiah 28:23-29. {CT 314.2}

God dispenses His gifts as it pleases Him. He bestows one gift upon one, and another gift upon another, but all for the good of the whole body. It is in God's order that some shall be of service in one line of work, and others in other lines--all working under the selfsame Spirit. The recognition of this plan will be a safeguard against emulation, pride, envy, or contempt of one another. It will strengthen unity and mutual love. {CT 314.3}

A much larger number of young people need to have the advantages of our schools. They need the manual training course, which will teach them how to live an active, energetic life. Under wise, judicious, God-fearing directors, the students are to be taught different kinds of labor. Every branch of the work is to be conducted in the most thorough, systematic way that long experience and wisdom can enable us to plan and execute. {CT 315.1}

Let the teachers wake up to the importance of this subject, and teach agriculture and the other industries that it is essential for the students to understand. Let them seek in every department of labor to reach the very best results. Let the science of the word of God be brought into the work, that the students may understand correct principles and may reach the highest possible standard. {CT 315.2}

I urge that our schools be given encouragement in their efforts to develop plans for the training of the youth in agricultural and other lines of industrial work. When, in ordinary business, pioneer work is done and preparation is made for future development, there is frequently a financial loss. But let us remember the blessing that physical exercise brings to the students. Many students have died while endeavoring to acquire an education, because they confined themselves too closely to mental effort. {CT 317.1}

We must not be narrow in our plans. In industrial training there are unseen advantages which cannot be measured or estimated. Let no one begrudge the effort necessary to carry forward successfully the plan that for years has been urged upon us as of primary importance. {CT 317.2}

God has revealed to me that we are in positive danger of bringing into our educational work the customs and fashions that prevail in the schools of the world. If teachers are not guarded, they will place on the necks of their students worldly yokes instead of the yoke of Christ. The plan of the schools we shall establish in these closing years of the message is to be of an entirely different order from those we have instituted. {CT 532.2}

For this reason, God bids us establish schools away from the cities, where, without let or hindrance, we can carry on the education of students upon plans that are in harmony with the solemn message committed to us for the world. Such an education as this can best be worked out where there is land to cultivate and where the physical exercise taken by the students can be of such a nature as to act a valuable part in their character building and fit them for usefulness in the fields to which they shall go. {CT 532.3}

God will bless those schools that are conducted according to His design. When we were laboring to establish the educational work in Australia, the Lord revealed to us that this school must not pattern after any schools that had been established in the past. This was to be a sample school. It was organized on the plan that God had given us, and He has prospered its work. {CT 533.1}

I have been shown that in our educational work we are not to follow the methods that have been adopted in our older established schools. There is among us too much clinging to old customs, and because of this we are far behind where we should be in the development of the third angel's message. Because men could not comprehend the purpose of God in the plans laid before us for the education of workers, methods have been followed in some of our schools which have retarded rather than advanced the work of God. Years have passed into eternity with small results, that might have shown the accomplishment of a great work. If the Lord's will had been done by the workers in earth as the angels do it in heaven, much that now remains to be done would be already accomplished, and noble results would be seen as the fruit of missionary effort. {CT 533.2}

The usefulness learned on the school farm is the very education that is most essential for those who go out as missionaries to many foreign fields. If this training is given with the glory of God in view, great results will be seen. No work will be more effectual than that done by those who, having obtained an education in practical life, go forth to mission fields with the message of truth, prepared to instruct as they have been instructed. The knowledge they have obtained in the tilling of the soil and other lines of manual work, and which they carry with them to their fields of labor, will make them a blessing even in heathen lands.--Special Testimonies, Series B, No. 11 pp. 27-30. {CT 534.1}

July 15, 1913

Particular directions were given of God in regard to the manner of observing the Sabbath. All unnecessary work was strictly forbidden, and the day before the Sabbath was made a day of preparation, that everything might be in readiness for its sacred hours. "This is that which the Lord hath said, Tomorrow is the rest of the holy Sabbath unto the Lord: bake that which ye will bake today, and seethe that ye will seethe; and that which remaineth over lay up for you to be kept until the morning." {ST, July 15, 1913 par. 1}

The Israelites were not in any case to do their own work on the Sabbath. The divine direction was, "Six days thou shalt work, but on the seventh day thou shalt rest: in earing time and in harvest thou shalt rest." In the busiest seasons of the year, when their fruits and grains were to be secured, they were to remember that their temporal blessings came from the bountiful hand of their Creator, and He could increase or diminish them according to their faithfulness or unfaithfulness in His service. {ST, July 15, 1913 par. 2}

The Lord places a high estimate upon His Sabbath. Through His prophet He has promised: "If thou turn away thy foot from the Sabbath, from doing thy pleasure on My holy day; and call the Sabbath a delight, the holy of the Lord, honorable; and shalt honor Him, not doing thine own ways, nor finding thine own pleasure, nor speaking thine own words: then shalt thou delight thyself in the Lord; and I will cause thee to ride upon the high places of the earth, and feed thee with the heritage of Jacob thy father: for the mouth of the Lord hath spoken it." {ST, July 15, 1913 par. 3}

With God there is no respect of persons. Those who fear Him and work righteousness are precious in His sight; but He requires His people to show their allegiance by strict obedience to all the precepts of the moral law, the Sabbath commandment with the rest. God is jealous of His honor, and let men beware how they remove one jot or tittle of that law that He spoke with His own voice and wrote with His own finger upon tables of stone, and that He has pronounced holy, just, and good. {ST, July 15, 1913 par. 4}

July 16, 1915 – Death of Ellen White

1916

The wall of Jerusalem had not yet been completed when Nehemiah's attention was called to the unhappy condition of the poorer classes of the people. In the unsettled state of the country, tillage had been to some extent neglected. Furthermore, because of the selfish course pursued by some who had returned to Judea, the Lord's blessing was not resting upon their land, and there was a scarcity of grain. {PK 646.1}

In order to obtain food for their families, the poor were obliged to buy on credit and at exorbitant prices. They were also compelled to raise money by borrowing on interest to pay the heavy taxes imposed upon them by the kings of Persia. To add to the distress of the poor, the more wealthy among the Jews had taken advantage of their necessities, thus enriching themselves. {PK 646.2}

The Lord had commanded Israel, through Moses, that every third year a tithe be raised for the benefit of the poor; and a further provision had been made in the suspension of agricultural labor every seventh year, the land lying fallow, its spontaneous products being left to those in need. Faithfulness in devoting these offerings to the relief of the poor and to other benevolent uses would have tended to keep fresh before the people the truth of God's ownership of all, and their opportunity to be channels of blessing. It was Jehovah's purpose that the Israelites should have a training that would eradicate selfishness, and develop breadth and nobility of character. {PK 646.3}

God had also instructed through Moses: "If thou lend money to any of My people that is poor by thee, thou shalt not be to him as an usurer." "Thou shalt not lend upon usury to thy brother; usury of money, usury of victuals, usury of anything that is lent upon usury." Exodus 22:25; Deuteronomy 23:19. Again He had said, "If there be among you a poor man of one of thy brethren within any of thy gates in thy land which the Lord thy God giveth thee, thou shalt not harden thine heart, nor shut thine hand from thy poor brother: but thou shalt open thine hand wide unto him, and shalt surely lend him sufficient for his need, in that which he wanteth." "For the poor shall never cease out of the land: therefore I command thee, saying, Thou shalt open thine hand wide unto thy brother, to thy poor, and to thy needy, in thy land." Deuteronomy 15:7, 8, 11. {PK 647.1}

Note: Though published after Ellen White's death, Prophets and Kings was finished prior to her death in 1915. It was her last major work.

Index

Education

End Time Motivations

End-Time Motivations

Farming and the Poor

Farming in Ancient Israel

God's Work

Health Work and Sanitariums